LAPSING INTO

A COMMA

A Curmudgeon's Guide
to the Many Things That Can Go Wrong in Print—
and How to Avoid Them

BILL WALSH

Copy Desk Chief

Busi

CB
CONTEMPORARY BOOKS

Library of Congress Cataloging-in-Publication Data

Walsh, Bill (William F.)
    Lapsing into a comma : a curmudgeon's guide to the many things that can go wrong in print—and how to avoid them / Bill Walsh.
        p.   cm.
    Includes index.
    ISBN 0-8092-2535-2
    1. Authorship—Style manuals.   2. Editing—Handbooks, manuals, etc.   3. English language—Style—Handbooks, manuals, etc.   I. Title.
PN147.W33   2000
808'.027—dc21
                                                                99-53468
                                                                CIP

Cover design by Monica Baziuk
Cover illustration by Dan Krovatin
Interior design by Jeanette Wojtyla

Published by Contemporary Books
A division of NTC/Contemporary Publishing Group, Inc.
4255 West Touhy Avenue, Lincolnwood (Chicago), Illinois 60712-1975 U.S.A.
Printed in the United States of America
International Standard Book Number: 0-8092-2535-2

00 01 02 03 04 05 LB 18 17 16 15 14 13 12 11 10 9 8 7 6 5 4 3 2 1

For Jacqueline, my bride

CONTENTS

Acknowledgments

This book would have been a heck of a lot tougher to write without the precedents set by a host of stylebooks before it, and I especially want to acknowledge my debt to the Associated Press Stylebook and Libel Manual. I had never heard of such a publication when I was handed a copy, along with a test, after I applied for my first editing job, a "copyreader" position at the University of Arizona's Arizona Daily Wildcat. I found that powder-blue spiral-bound paperback endlessly helpful and fascinating, and I got the job.

In this book I'm sharply critical of some AP style rulings, but no two usage arbiters agree on everything, and I continue to have an enormous respect for the AP manual as a comprehensive volume that takes a bold stab at the impossibly ambitious task of being all things to all papers. The Washington Post, the New York Times and other publications have fine stylebooks of their own, as do magazines and book publishers, but my discussion of style will begin with AP.

I'd also like to extend my gratitude to the copy chiefs and other editors who have nurtured my career, most recently Vince Rinehart at the Post but before that Barbara Taylor and John Wilson at the Washington Times, Alan Moran at the Phoenix Gazette, and Frank Miele and Tom Nichols at the Wildcat.

INTRODUCTION

I've been a journalist for 19 years now, and about 10 years ago I decided to make a point of jotting down every interesting style issue that came up. Often the issue was something not covered in the AP stylebook, the traditional newsroom bible. In other cases it was something covered in that stylebook but widely ignored by writers and copy editors—or something that exposed flaws in the stylebook's advice or in the conventional wisdom. These nuggets form the core of this book. I cover many of the usual bases (*a* vs. *an*, *that* vs. *which*), but I also address such arcana as why a right hook is a bad example of a punch and how to tell a Playmate from a Playboy Bunny.

I doubt you'll find my advice predictable. I mix traditionalism (never, ever, use *which* when you mean *that*) with a streak of liberalism (don't believe what you've heard about *hopefully*). I make a case for *media* as a singular noun, and I argue that using the active voice isn't always preferable.

I've framed this book as a usage manual for all writers and copy editors. While my experience is specifically as a

newspaper copy editor, in a way all literate people are copy
editors, whether they be writers rewriting their own work or
simply avid readers noticing a typo on a cereal box. And I've
been careful to note those style points that are specific to
newspapers.

I've used headings and, where possible, alphabetical order
to organize the contents of this book, but many entries cover
multiple topics. Any search for a specific topic should begin at
the back of the book, with the comprehensive index.

To write about usage is to tempt the gods and the gremlins, and so I fully expect this book to contain errors. If you
find one, please be gentle.

BEYOND SEARCH AND REPLACE

Using Your Head as Well as Your Stylebook

I've written a stylebook that I hope makes the following point: Be skeptical of stylebooks.

This is not to concede any lack of confidence in the logical grounding and overall good sense of this collection of fact and opinion. What I'm saying is that it's relatively easy to pick a stylebook, any stylebook, and learn the rules it imposes. It's harder to apply those rules correctly and consistently, and harder still to truly understand the reasons behind the rules—and therefore know when they should be ignored.

Memorizing the rules is fine when it comes to such things as the choice between *Road* and *Rd.* in addresses, but it tends to blunt the language's finer distinctions when applied to real, live prose. For example, most copy editors would tell you that *compare with* is used to examine differences and *compare to* is used to examine similarities—and they'd be wrong. This error comes from a misunderstanding of a real rule; some others result from the application of so-called rules that are really nothing more than superstitions. Combine the misunderstandings and the superstitions and you get copy editors who automatically change *different than* to *different from*, *which* to *that*, *have never* to *never have*, *convince* to *persuade*, *gender* to *sex*, *hopefully* to *it is to be hoped that*, *host* to *play host to*, *impact* to *effect*, *may* to *might*, passive voice to active voice, fragments to sentences.

These changes aren't always wrong, but they shouldn't be *automatic*. I call such an approach the search-and-replace school of copy editing, and I think it's largely responsible for the low esteem many writers have for editors—and for the misguided notion that spell-check and grammar-check software could easily replace copy editors.

Copy editors are there to enforce (a) correctness and (b) style. Correctness covers matters of fact and matters of grammar, usage and spelling, but it also covers clarity: Copy editors are supposed to make sure writers are actually saying what they think they're saying. Style rules keep you from saying *Inc.* and *Incorporated* in the same article, but they can be misused. In the hands of a tin-eared copy editor, a breezy reference to Ford having a better idea might become *Dearborn, Mich.-based Ford Motor Co. once claimed in television advertisements to have a better idea.* Not long ago, the Associated Press stylebook did not include Las Vegas among its "dateline cities"—those places that may be mentioned without specifying what state they're in—and more than once I saw *Las Vegas gambling* changed to *Las Vegas, Nev., gambling.*

You don't need an encyclopedic knowledge of grammatical terms to write and edit with precision. I couldn't diagram a sentence if my life depended on it. But I recognize that the phrase *Bill and Hillary Rodham Clinton* invents a nonexistent person named *Bill Rodham Clinton* (you have to say either *Bill and Hillary Clinton* or *Bill Clinton and Hillary Rodham Clinton*) and that *the Gaza Strip and West Bank town of Jericho* places Jericho in both the West Bank and the Gaza Strip (*West Bank* needs its own *the*). A finely tuned ear is at least as important as formal grammar, and that's not something you can acquire by memorizing a stylebook. But reading and thinking about a stylebook writer's reasoning might help you develop that ear. That's why I wrote this book.

You Could Look It Up!

How to Use a Dictionary With Style

At most publications and publishing companies, a stylebook (such as the Associated Press stylebook or the Chicago Manual of Style) is the primary arbiter of usage, with a specified dictionary (Webster's New World College Dictionary, for publications and publishers that follow AP style) as the secondary source. A well-stocked copy desk will also have a depth-charge-size unabridged dictionary and some specialized glossaries. You can also find these at any library.

Here's how these players fit into the lineup:

Say you're writing or editing for a publication that uses AP style and you want to know whether *tabletop* is one word or two. You pick up the stylebook and find that *tabletop* is not listed. So you turn to Webster's New World, and the word isn't there either. Problem solved: It's *table top*. Many conscientious writers and editors make the mistake of scurrying over to the "big" dictionary at this point, but that's not the big dictionary's role. Assuming the primary dictionary contains both *table* and *top*, its lack of a *tabletop* entry is as good as an entry saying the noun is spelled *table top*. (The adjective is a different story; there your hyphenation policy comes into play.) The big dictionary, the medical dictionary and the dictionary of World War I-era German aircraft parts should be reserved for obscure terms whose components cannot be found in the primary sources.

Dictionaries won't always offer a definitive word on spellings, but for style purposes only one spelling is "correct." If two spellings are listed, go with the first one. If a word spelled one way is defined as the same word spelled another way, the latter is correct style (look up *grey* and the dictionary will say *GRAY*, meaning *gray* is correct). More troublesome are entries that read "usually" or "often." With Webster's New World, it's best to treat the "usually" and "often" entries as correct.

COMPOUNDS
What the Dictionary Doesn't Always Tell You

A common mistake is to glance at a dictionary or stylebook entry without noting which part of speech is being described. I've seen *She got a makeover* changed to *She got a make over* many times, because Webster's New World lists *make over*. A closer look shows that *make over* is listed only as a verb; this is a bad omission, but the basic rules of compound formation mean such nouns cannot possibly be two words; if they aren't one word, they're hyphenated (*make-over*). Similarly, this dictionary lists the verb *start up* but is silent on the noun, which therefore has to be *start-up*.

Compounds are formed differently with the different parts of speech:

Compound nouns follow no particular logic. Check your stylebook and your dictionary of choice, and if a compound isn't listed in either, then it's two words—unless it's a verb-plus-preposition formation (more on that later).

The standard line is that over time two-word compounds evolve into hyphenates and then into single words. This is true to some extent, but the hyphen stage (as in the "ice-berg" that sank the Titanic) is seldom seen nowadays, and plenty of long-lived compounds remain two words in today's dictionaries. *Ballplayer* is a legitimate word, but you'll never see *baseballplayer* or *footballplayer*—they're just too long and awkward. I feel the same way about *copyeditor*, but many of my colleagues, especially in the non-newspaper publishing world, disagree. (Perhaps they've yedited too many cops.) Novelist and essayist Nicholson Baker, in his book "The Size of Thoughts," tells of restoring the space in a *back seat* that his copy editor had changed to *backseat*, his reasoning being that *back seat* more accurately reflects the pronunciation, in which both sides of the compound get equal stress. The pronunciation test isn't always reliable, but it's an important factor to keep in mind when evaluating whether a compound's migration from two words to one makes any sense. Note the one-syllable stress in *backache*, *backbeat*, *backbite* and *backhand* compared with the stress on both words in *back seat*, *back pain*

and *back taxes*. *Back yard* (noun) and *backyard* (adjective) illustrate the point well: Say out loud "I'm having a backyard barbecue in my back yard" and note the pronunciation difference.

With a few exceptions, mainly in the area of slang (you
won't find *scumbag* in many dictionaries, but it's obviously a
solid coinage), you should defer to the established reference
sources and not take it upon yourself to hasten the solidifica-
tion of a compound.

Verb-plus-preposition compound nouns must be either solid or
hyphenated. Check your stylebook and dictionary, and if you
don't find the word as solid, use the hyphen. When something
is made over, it's a *make-over*; when something is built up, it's
a *buildup*; when someone is knocked down, it's a *knockdown*;
when someone breaks in, it's a *break-in*; when you print something out, you get a *printout*. It amazes me to see that some
otherwise literate people are willing to accept *print out* as a
noun, as in "I got a print out." If *printout* isn't in your dictionary, then it becomes *print-out*, but under no circumstances
should this kind of compound noun remain two words. *Print*
and *out* work together; *print* isn't an adjective that modifies the
noun *out*. This is a very simple concept, but it's not easy to
explain to those who don't get it right away.

Compound verbs should be hyphenated:

> *Holyfield head-butted his opponent.*
> *I copy-edited the story.*
> *She pole-vaulted.*

Compound modifiers, also known as *unit modifiers* or *compound
adjectives*, generally must be hyphenated. A victory on the

home field is a *home-field victory*. In a few cases, compounds that are two words in the noun form become solid as an adjective (a shed in the back yard is a *backyard shed*), but this kind of marriage should be performed only when it's explicitly prescribed by your stylebook or dictionary. There are exceptions to the hyphenate-all-compound-modifiers rule. For example, you shouldn't stick hyphens within a single proper noun (*a White House source*) or a single expression contained in quotation marks (*a "win at all costs" attitude*). Foreign-language phrases also stick together just fine without hyphens (*the ad hoc committee*), and stylebooks generally, and wisely, leave out hyphens in percentages and dollar amounts (*the 2 percent tax increase will eliminate a $75 million deficit*).

And now for the sticky part: Virtually every editor makes at least some exceptions for readily recognized compounds that often act as modifiers. You'll seldom see a hyphen in *high school graduate* or *Clinton administration officials*, for example, and many editors extend this exception to *ice cream cone, real estate agent, law enforcement officer, health care plan* and the like.

Still other editors, many of whom seem to have a phobia when it comes to hyphens, enforce a rule that eliminates the hyphen from modifiers unless doing so would result in confusion. No one would think *orange juice salesmen* means juice salesmen who are orange, they reason, and therefore the hyphen isn't necessary. Personally, I think people in the latter camp don't understand the concept of hyphens. Sure, *orange juice salesmen* isn't going to be confusing in its entirety, but for one nanosecond the reader is going to be led down the wrong path, thinking *orange* is the modifier and *juice* is the noun, only to be hit with another noun and forced to backtrack to mentally link *orange* and *juice*. The job of an editor is to make things as easy as possible on the reader, and the least an editor could do is stick in a little hyphen and make that link to begin with.

Longer-than-two-word compound adjectives frighten even those who aren't afraid of orange-juice salesmen, but the same rules apply. A two-word modifier gets one hyphen, a three-word modifier gets two hyphens, and a 27-word modifier gets 26 hyphens.

Of course, the need for multiple hyphens (*anti-capital-gains-tax-cut forces*, for example) is often a cry for help ("Rewrite!"), unless it's a string-a-lot-of-words-together-for-comic-effect sort of thing. If you write that *the upscale town house market is booming*, you deserve to be stabbed with a couple of hyphens (*the upscale-town-house market is booming*). Why not *the market for upscale town houses is booming*?

Rewrite, by all means, if you hate hyphens (*those opposed to a cut in the capital-gains tax*, for example), but what you must not do is arbitrarily decide to disconnect the unit by using only the most obvious hyphen and ditching the rest. Hyphenation is often an all-or-nothing proposition: Even if you eschew the hyphen when *high school* is a modifier (*high school students*), you cannot apply that logic when that modifier gains an addition. *High school-age students* means "school-age students who are under the influence of drugs." It's *high-school-age students*. Don't be afraid. The hyphens won't gang up and attack you.

The all-or-nothing linkage principle is especially crucial when prefixes and suffixes are involved. Consider the vast difference between an *anti-child-abuse program* and an *anti-child abuse program*.

A related issue is how to handle phrases such as *the 1.1-million-member union*. Again, I think two hyphens are needed to hold things together, but lots of publications would leave off the first one in this example. Bad style decision, I'd say, but you couldn't really call it wrong.

Some publications use the *en dash*, a dash wider than a hyphen but narrower than a regular, or *em*, dash, as a substitute for repeated hyphens—*high school–age boys, 1.1 million–member union*—but I'm not a fan of this solution (see Page 84).

When a compound modifier is used after the term it modifies (I hate these labels, but I believe that would make it a *compound predicate adjective*), you can sometimes skip the hyphen. You might call someone *a well-read scholar*, but turn that around and the hyphen disappears: *a scholar who is well read. Reddish-brown hair*, styled differently, becomes *hair that is reddish brown*. Some authorities would leave out the hyphen in *all* such cases, but I disagree. You'll have to use your judgment and your ear, but it should be clear that while some phrases acquire hyphens when they're placed before a term they modify, others already came with the hyphens and should never lose them. A book that is easy to read is *an easy-to-read book*: The phrase *easy to read* occurs naturally without hyphens but sprouts those hyphens in the modifier role. But *fat-free yogurt* is never hyphen-free: *Fat-free*, like *self-made* and *hard-working*, was born as a modifier, hyphen and all. The *-free* part is more suffix than word, and to describe someone as *hard working* borders on unreadable.

Commingling compounds (a term I just made up) are a good test of a writer or editor's facility with the language. For example, there is gunfire and there are submachine guns, but there's no such thing as *submachine gunfire*. Take a good look at the term and separate the noun from the modifier. The modifier *gun* in the noun *gunfire* is also a noun that's being modified by *submachine*, leaving *fire* as the true noun in the equation. So *gun* must go where it's needed most and the compound must be *submachine-gun fire*, just as we write *small-business man* and *elementary-school teacher* instead of *small businessman* and *elementary schoolteacher*. It's the gun that's submachine, not the gunfire; it's the business that's small, not (necessarily) the man; and it's the school that's elementary, not (again, necessarily) the teacher.

HOLDING THE (VIRTUAL) FORT

Disturbing Trends in the Information Age

"We must resist the temptation to turn the language into one long word," a former editor of mine once wrote in vetoing AP style on *airstrike*. Since then, *cellphones* and *videogames* and *websites* and—I can barely bring myself to type this—*email* have blitzed us with the suggestion that English should be more like German, in which adjectives merge with the nouns they modify to create new words. The techies who brought us the point-and-click wonderland of the Internet are brilliant people, but they're not the ones we should be looking to for language instruction.

The way things work in *English*, as I pointed out in Chapter 2, is that compound nouns evolve over time from two words, and possibly the hyphenated form, before crystallizing into a single word. This works in a semi-democratic fashion, with all literate writers of the language weighing in while newspapers, books and magazines lay down the law. Dictionaries and major stylebooks act as the judge and jury. Before the computer age, we had a conservative judicial branch. This can be a good thing: It keeps fads from littering the language (if the Internet is replaced by direct-broadcast-to-brain technology tomorrow, *website* will soon look as silly as *draftdodging* and *braburning* and *goldfishswallowing*). It can also keep prose looking rather quaint, however, as when AP mandates *town house*, *hot line* and *teen-ager* for the words that have been *townhouse*, *hotline* and *teenager* in the real world for at least 25 years.

But today, it seems, compounds that few people had heard of five years ago are merging instantly into one-word terms. Even AP accepts *online*, a development that might make sense in isolation—you could argue that the catchall term for this phenomenon that is taking over the world deserves an accelerated evolution from the ad hoc *on line* (adv.) and *on-line* (adj.)—but is alarmingly inconsistent for a stylebook that still embraces the hoary *hot line*. Once-thoughtful editors who lapse into such inconsistencies in a blind rush to stay "current" remind me of parents who raise their first or second child with strict rules but take a permissive "Oh, the hell with it!" approach to the newer arrivals. At least the parents can say "Well, times have changed—if we were raising kid number one today we'd be doing the same things we're doing now." These editors, on the other hand, are still actively repressing the older kids, and one of them is a *teenager*.

When Evolution Is Legitimate

You might be tempted to think at this point that I'm a white-haired Luddite. I'm neither. I'm not yet 40, and I built a Web site from scratch—raw HTML, no helper software—in early 1995, before the vast majority of Americans had ever heard of the World Wide Web. I've absorbed countless Internet-related terms as the technology behind them first became available to the public. Whereas the publishing industry's later arrivals to the on-line world might have felt like outsiders in an already flourishing civilization with a well-developed language of its own, I know firsthand just how flimsy the linguistic foundations of that civilization actually were. I was introduced to *Web site*, *home page* and *e-mail*, and so I know that *website*, *homepage* and *email* came about as shortcuts or just plain errors, as opposed to a gospel laid down by the creators of the Internet.

This isn't to say that cyberspeak contains no legitimate one-word coinages. There—I just used one! *Cyber-*, as a prefix, can legitimately be attached to words. Just as *bio-* gave us *biotech*, *cyber-* has given us *cyberspace*, *cybercafes* and countless other terms. And you might be surprised to learn that I consider *newsgroup* a correct term for Usenet discussion areas. Even though *news* and *group* are perfectly good words, the whole of *newsgroup* is greater than—or at least different from—the sum of its parts. While a Web site is a site on the Web, and a home page is a page of the home variety, newsgroups can't really be described as news groups. They aren't necessarily about news, and their free-for-all nature belies the sense of membership implied by *group*.

And I'm not far from being swayed on *online*. Although I continue to defend the reasoning behind *on-line* and *on line*,

I admit that they are starting to collect a patina of quaintness. I will repeat, however, that *online* should be used only by publications progressive enough to have already accepted such things as *hotline, townhouse* and *teenager*.

E-GADS!

When the shortened form of *electronic mail* first began appearing in print, the question was whether it should be *e-mail* or *E-mail*; the lowercase form has clearly prevailed, although using the uppercase would be an acceptable style decision.

My faith in human intelligence still hasn't recovered from the development that followed: The predominant spelling among the general public has become *email*, which is an abomination. No initial-based term in the history of the English language has ever evolved to form a solid word—a few are split, and the rest are hyphenated. Look at *A-frame, B-movie, C-rations, D-Day, E-* (uh, skip that one), *F layer, G-string, H-bomb, I-beam, J-school, K car, L-shaped, N-word, O-ring, Q rating, S-connector, T-shirt, U-boat, X-ray, Y-chromosome, Z particle* and scores of other such compounds. It doesn't even *look* right; at first glance, the *e* in *email* begs to be pronounced unaccented, as a schwa (*"uh-MAIL"*). Setting the letter apart makes it clear that the letter is a letter and that the one-letter syllable is accented. E! E! Eeeeeee!

But an AltaVista search of the Web shows that ignorance is taking over: *Uhmail* outnumbers *e-mail* by more than two to one. The dictionaries, if you believe their "descriptive, not prescriptive" mantra ("We *reflect* usage; we don't dictate it"), cannot be far behind.

HOW DID THIS HAPPEN?

I find it hard to fathom how anyone ever *thought* of writing *email*, but a good guess is that the speed-is-everything informality of e-mail itself, with its minimalist punctuation as well as its lack of capital letters, is the culprit. People who knew better started using it for speed's sake, and then those late adopters who ain't big on book learnin' started seeing *email* in their e-mail without ever having seen the correct term. It's as if technology has somehow "solved" the problem of slow linguistic evolution, and in an insidious way that's true. Whereas in the old days people had only (professionally edited) newspapers, magazines and books from which to take their usage cues, in the Internet world everyone's a publisher. This is a wonderful development in many ways. If you have something to say, you can say it to a mass audience. If you're a huge fan of the second-best Bulgarian in women's tennis, you're not likely to find her biography at Borders—whereas the World Wide Web might have encyclopedic, illustrated sites devoted to her. But if everyone's a publisher, can everyone afford an editor? Of course not. Internet discourse is unfiltered, and in losing the filter that blocks material without mass appeal, we also lose the filters that separate fact from fiction and standard from substandard language. The power of the usage police has been significantly diluted.

Before the Internet became a mass medium, it was difficult to assess just how large the gap between "correct" English and popular usage was. Today it's clear and it's frightening. More than half a million Web pages mention nude pictures of "amature" models. While this output doesn't equal that of correct-spelling pornographers, the margin isn't much—fewer than 2 million pages talk of *amateur* nudes. These people have access to spell-check, mind you, and that word won't exactly be found alongside *supersede*, *tendinitis* and *idiosyncrasy* on the spelling-bee list. Another fun search-engine exercise is to see how many Web sites—some of which are devoted to "worshiping" her—misspell the name of actress Courteney Cox Arquette. An AltaVista search finds at least eight spellings of her first name.

But our focus here is compounds, and if there's one thing the average civilian will screw up more often than not, it's the distinction between one word and two. One of my guilty pleasures on the Web is reading Las Vegas trip reports. Several sites publish gambling pilgrims' minute-by-minute diaries, and you can be sure they'll contain sentences like "I wanted to get me some primerib, but they says there ain't no bare foot people allowed in the buffetline."

That might explain how *email* and *homepage* and *website* became part of the informal vernacular, but why are such things seeping into respectable publications? Well, a large segment of the otherwise intelligent grown-up population is afraid of computers, and that "Oh, dear, I might break something" hands-off approach has translated to the *language* of computing as well. Just as some people are afraid to touch computers, out of fear that they might accidentally hit the "kill all documents" key, they're afraid to monkey with Internet terms or Internet companies' names. Perhaps it's an age thing: By the time these terms register on the radar of the people with the experience and authority to enforce the language's most basic rules, the terms have already been corrupted by the geek crowd. (Or is it *geekcrowd*?)

Am I being elitist? Sure I am. If you want to know how justin4326@aol.com spells things, look in an on-line chat room. If you're interested in what's correct, at least for now, in the ever-evolving area of usage, you have to pick up a dictionary or a usage book. Dictionary editors insist that they only reflect usage, but that's a lie they use to fend off the anti-elitist "no rights, no wrongs" contingent, just as art snobs snicker at the "I don't know anything about art, but I know what I like" joke while keeping a long list of things we're not allowed to like. If dictionaries really reflected usage, we'd be eating "sherbert."

UPS AND DOWNS

An even more disturbing trend is the migration of vanity orthography—the fancying-up of logos and the like with creative capitalization (or the lack thereof) and cutesy symbols—from the world of marketing, where it is perfectly appropriate, to the text of newspapers, magazines and books.

Sentences and proper nouns begin with capital letters. Words are all caps only when they're acronyms—when each letter stands for another word. At the risk of sounding like Robert Fulghum, everything we needed to know about capitalization we learned in . . . well, maybe second grade.

But people don't trust these simple rules anymore. They all laughed when Sarah Jessica Parker's character in the movie "L.A. Story" gave her name as "SanDeE*," but now this crap is being taken seriously. The dot-com era has leveled a wall that Adidas and K.D. Lang and "Thirtysomething" had already cracked, and suddenly writers and editors faced with a name are asking "Is that capitalized?"—a question that's about as appropriate as asking a 5-year-old "Do you want that Coke with or without rum?"

ARBITRARY CAPITALIZATION
After playing Chess, let's have a Turkey Sandwich

Show me most anybody's resume, most any restaurant menu, most any personal Web site, and I'm likely to cringe at a phenomenon I call *arbitrary capitalization.*

It's not really arbitrary; in fact, there's usually a pretty well-defined logic to it. It's almost like the German language, in which all nouns are capitalized. Arbitrary cappers don't cap all nouns, but they do cap the nouns they consider important:

> *I studied Ballet for two years.*
> *His passion was Chess.*
> *Prime Rib of Beef served with a*
> *Beurre Blanc sauce.*
> *He majored in Omnipresence and*
> *minored in Philately.*

There's nothing particularly evil about all this, and I would like to believe most of the perpetrators know deep down that it's wrong.

Beurre blanc is white butter; it's not White Butter. (Cap'n John's Rootin' Tootin' Make-Your-Eyeballs-Explode Crab Seasoning, to pull one example from thin air, would be another matter altogether.) And philately (well, let's make that engineering) is a subject, a field of study, an endeavor. That doesn't make it a proper noun. Now, Engineering 101 would make sense capitalized, as a course title. So would Fundamentals of Engineering or even Advanced Engineering, though the latter would have to be very clearly stated as a course title to avoid raising my eyebrow.

On the Web, I came across an author's fascinating account of the gory details of getting a book published. In an otherwise well-founded rant about ham-handed work by a copy editor, he writes, "She bashed 'the Space Shuttle' down to 'the space shuttle' instead of visiting www .nasa.gov." Uh, right, pal—let's take *all* our usage cues from the federal government. NASA also capitalizes *Astronauts*, just as the Frito-Lay site capitalizes *Potato Chips*. The appeal-to-authority fallacy won't win you a capital letter.

continued

> To review, capital letters (aside from sentence beginnings, titles, up-style headlines and the like) are reserved for proper nouns. And you know how testy I get about lowercased proper nouns.
>
> I must confess, by the way, that as a member of the Ironic Postmodern Generation, I tend to capitalize Grand Concepts, which usually translates to Concepts That Aren't Really Grand but Pretend to Be. This habit, annoying as it may be, has *Nothing to Do* with arbitrary capitalization.

Just about everything has a nonstandard logo. Look around you: "CANADA DRY SELTZER," "annie hall," "Entertainment WEEKLY," "*The* AMERICAN HERITAGE *dic•tion•ar•y of* THE ENGLISH LANGUAGE." Sure, the credits say "thirtysomething," but the credits also say "DRAGNET" and "THREE'S COMPANY." These variations, employed in advertising and packaging, add visual interest to our world. Carry these variations over to print journalism, however, and they bring the look of a cheesy press release. Back when all-caps logos were common but all-lowercase ones were rare, grown-ups with typewriters reflexively followed the basic rules of capitalization. But *e.e. cummings* and then *adidas* and then "*thirtysomething*" and *k.d. lang* stood out, and writers and editors gradually got down and boogied. The all-caps logos "DANCES WITH WOLVES" and HEINZ TOMATO KETCHUP weren't deemed worthy of replicating, but writers in an increasingly acronym-and-abbreviation-filled world began to mistake short, snappy words for acronyms (*FAX*), and if a short, snappy product name happened to have an all-caps logo, up it went (*NIKE, VISA*).

K.D. Lang and "*Thirtysomething*" and *Adidas* and *Nike* are the names of a singer, a TV show and a couple of shoe companies, and as writers and editors it's our job to report these names. It's not our job to replicate their logos—the color, the point size, the typeface or, yes, the creative capitalization.

In many, perhaps most, cases, these logo affectations aren't even *intended* to indicate the preferred style for proper names. E.E. Cummings, for example, used capital letters in his signature. I might sound like a lonely voice on this issue, but Tennis magazine and, believe it or not, Amazon.com illustrate the way capitalization is supposed to work in the grown-up world. For more than 20 years, Tennis magazine was *tennis* on the cover (it only recently dropped the mod '70s logo) and *TENNIS* in its own articles (a lot of publications like self-referential caps)—but *Tennis* in real life. And those writers who try to be oh-so-modern and oh-so-accommodating by writing "amazon.com" might want to double-check the way the on-line bookstore refers to itself outside logo-land (and even in some of its myriad logo styles). That's right: It's *Amazon.com*.

Sometimes, even more strangely, a company adopts an odd style for its name that *doesn't* reflect its logo. The telephone company US West has a funky smushed-together US*WEST* logo, but it reports its name in more official contexts as *U S West*. That's right: There's a space between those initials, as in *U* [dramatic pause] *S West.* Start humoring the US West people on that and they'll start quibbling about the exact dimensions of their precious space. Nip it in the bud.

.COM WHAT MAY

All Web sites have addresses, but most of them have *names* as well, and it can be confusing when the twain meet. The site named Amazon.com can be found at the address http:// www.amazon.com. Web addresses should be printed all lowercase, in accordance with Web convention, when they're listed for readers' convenience, but they should never be treated as names. If a site has no name, describe it briefly and include the address as an aside: *The photos can be found at Harvey Baxter's Web site (http://www.access.digex.net/~hbaxter/ home.html).* If a site's name and its address (or at least an address that "points" to the correct site) are identical, use the name and therefore the capital letter—the site name is Barnesandnoble.com, despite the lowercase *b* in the logo. If you're worried that the capital letter will throw off surfers looking for the site, don't be: Internet domain names are not case-sensitive. I'm not sure who's more responsible for all this lowercasing—youngsters trying to be hip or oldsters so computer-shy they're afraid a capital letter might crash the Internet.

EASY ON THE EYES

The basic capitalization rules aren't arbitrary constructs; they're readers' helpers. Scan a wordy paragraph to quickly find out who or what is being written about and you seek out capital letters. Lowercased proper nouns can leave readers confused as well as jarred: Publications that indulge writer Bell Hooks's preference for the lowercase had better be ready to explain what bell hooks are.

I have no problem with the midstream caps in smushed-together names such as *NationsBank* and *CompuServe* (*bank* and *serve* are actual words), and another exception that I can grudgingly live with is the use of a lowercased letter or two immediately followed by a capital, as in *eBay* and *iMac*. The lowercasing actually means something (a play on Internet conventions), and at least there's a cap *near* the start of the word. If you start *de Gaulle* and *van Gogh* with lowercase letters, this isn't much of a stretch. Keep in mind, however, that sentence beginnings and the like remain capitalized. If you'd use capital letters in the headline *Man Bites Dog*, then you have to do the same with *EBay Gains Popularity*.

Another reader-unfriendly device that is fine in logos but not in names is false-alarm end-of-sentence punctuation. If I'm reading along and I see a reference to Guess? jeans, I don't get to the *jeans*. I stop at *Guess?* and try to figure out the answer to the question. At the end of a sentence it's even worse, as the sentence will look like a genuine question. The logo is *GUESS?*, but the name is *Guess*. If a newspaper indulges Yahoo's preference for *Yahoo!*, it risks sounding way too excited in headlines (*Tech Stock Surge Boosts Yahoo!*).

The on-line brokerage whose logo is E*TRADE presents a difficult decision. It shouldn't be printed as all caps, of course, but what about that asterisk? I choose to treat it as a stylized hyphen and write *E-Trade*. While it's true that the asterisk is right there on the keyboard and all newspapers can reproduce it, I think it crosses the line from punctuation into

decoration. Plenty of companies use decorative elements that
many newspapers would not be able to reproduce, such as bul-
lets of various shapes, diamonds and even five-sided stars (as
in the stylized apostrophe in the Macy's logo). Similarly, the
Arkansas Democrat-Gazette in Little Rock is the *Arkansas
Democrat [insert funky seal here] Gazette* in its flag but uses the
hyphen in copy.

PREFERENTIAL TREATMENT?

Finally, bowing to the preferences of companies and people
when it comes to oddball capitalization and symbols might
look fine when you're dealing with "Yahoo!" and "k.d. lang,"
but what about the little guys? The aforementioned Bell "bell
hooks" Hooks isn't a household name in most households. And
to move further down the food chain, are you willing to enter-
tain the whims of every man in every street when publishing
a routine man-in-the-street story? If I could be guaranteed
that a gender-bending Canadian torch-twang-pop star would
be the only person ever to be associated with the all-lowercase conceit, I'd be inclined to cap and let cap. But people are
weird, and they're not getting any less so. It won't be long
before reporters start submitting man-on-the-street quotes
from "john smith." Still OK with you? How about another
ordinary citizen, perhaps being mentioned tiny type in the
back of the sports section for finishing 97th in a 10K race,
who insists that his name is I'M!!!A!!!NEAT!!GUY!!? You see,
the thing about this issue is that it's impossible to be a consistent liberal—you have to draw the line somewhere, and I
choose to draw it quicker than most. Let's say some states'-
rights kook decides that he wants to be known as John Q.

Alabamaalaskaarizonaarkansascaliforniacoloradoconnecticut-
delawaredistrictofcolumbiafloridageorgiahawaiiidahoillinois-
indianaiowakansaskentuckylouisianamainemarylandmassa-
chusettsmichiganminnesotamississippimissourimontana-
nebraskanevadanewhampshirenewjerseynewmexiconewyork-
northcarolinanorthdakotaohiooklahomaoregonpennsylvania-
rhodeislandsouthcarolinasouthdakotatennesseetexasutah-
vermontvirginiawashingtonwestvirginiawisconsinwyoming—
and that, furthermore, any abbreviation of that, even in headlines, constitutes an insult to his religious beliefs. I doubt any
publication would expend the ink, paper and trouble necessary
to honor that request. And as for Yahoo (!), would the pro-
exclamation-point faction be willing to extend the same
respect to obscure products that also use that punctuation?
My stereo speakers say *Cerwin-Vega!*—is that something you
want to spring on readers who have never heard that name,
especially in a passing reference? Are you prepared to start
footnoting all these oddities? And did you know that the Ann
Taylor chain of upscale women's clothing stores uses a period
in its smushed-together logo? If you accept *Guess?* and *Yahoo!*,
you are beholden to allow things like *Shoppers mobbed the
AnnTaylor. store in search of last-minute gifts*. Activist groups
like to combine inappropriate capital letters with exclamation
points, but again we must translate these names into standard
English. *STOP! The Violence* should be published as *Stop the
Violence*. And we should stop this nonsense.

CALL IT UNINATI

*The United Nations' Initial Assault
on the Language*

I'm about to start ranting about the United Nations. No, I'm not a right-winger up in arms about "one world government." What I am is a literate person fed up with stupid fake acronyms such as *UNSCOM* and *UNPROFOR*.

How difficult is it to determine a set of initials? If your best friend in kindergarten was Jimmy Carruthers, you might have called him J.C. Or, heck, you might have been creative enough to bypass the initial route and come up with a cool-sounding diminutive, such as *Jimcar*. But even at age 5 you'd know the difference between Jimcar and his initials.

Show little Jimmy to the geniuses at the United Nations and they'd be likely to tag him with an "acronym" like *JICARRUT*.

Once upon a time, perhaps in the Dag Hammarskjold era, this organization attracted the best and the brightest—people who could figure out that a good short version of *United Nations* might be, oh, I dunno, *U.N.*

UNESCO and *UNICEF* are true acronyms. *UNHCR* is a misguided mouthful that stands for a stupid name, but at least it truly *stands* for that name, the United Nations High Commissioner for Refugees.

Today, however, the United Nations pays staffers (handsomely, no doubt) to decide that the United Nations Special Commission (another stupid name, but I digress) is not *UNSC*, but *UNSCOM*. The United Nations Professional Force is not *UNPF*, but *UNPROFOR*. If today's U.N. people had formed the U.N., it would probably be called *UNNAT*, or maybe *UNITNA* or *UNINATI*.

It might not be so bad if these things were mellifluous, but *UNSCOM* and *UNPROFOR* don't exactly roll off the tongue (I still don't know how the latter is even pronounced). It might not be so bad if these monstrosities were treated the way a kindergartner would treat *Jim-car*, but the U.N. staff writers. (*UNSTAWRI*,

continued

right?) use all caps, as if the *U* and the *N* and the *S* and the *C* and the *O* and the *M* and the *U* and the *N* and the *P* and the *R* and the *O* and the *F* and the *O* and the *R* each stood for something.

My policy: Don't use these terms. Write *the U.N. representatives in Iraq* or whatever. If someone uses one of these terms in a quote, cap the first letter only: *Unscom, Unprofor.*

And if the UNITNA folks ever come to my door asking for a dime in the name of stamping out illiteracy, I'm afraid I'll have to say I gave at THOFIC (the office).

LITERALLY SPEAKING

Write What You Mean,
Mean What You Write

Don't lie to the reader. If journalism has a Hippocratic Oath, this is it. Most violations of this canon aren't deliberate untruths; they're symptoms of the same odd tendency that causes most of the common-sense-defying feats I'm railing against here: Reporters and editors think they can get away with not reporting and not editing because readers have some strange telepathic ability to get beyond their prose and into their craniums.

TRUE OR FALSE?

My desk at the Washington Times was once presented with a graphic that purported to list mutual funds that require "no minimum investment." A copy editor pointed out that this is highly unlikely; it might be a *low* minimum requirement, but it's hard to imagine walking into the offices of the Steadfast Amalgamated Pleistocene Hirsute Growth Fund and plunking down a penny or a dollar or even $100 and not being told to get lost.

Then again, it's *possible*, which is why we put the question to an editor who should have known the answer. Instead of checking it out, however, he pretty much agreed that those examples disproved the text but insisted that readers would read it "within the bounds of reality."

There's sometimes a fine line between constructive nit-picking and turning into Greg from the "Exact Words" episode of "The Brady Bunch," but I don't think this is even a close call. *No minimum* means "no minimum."

To use another TV reference, I'm reminded of the Monty Python sketch about cannibalism in the Royal Navy, in which one officer says, "And when we say there is none, we mean there is a certain amount."

Outside of obvious attempts at humor, it's not a good idea to write something that you don't intend to be taken seriously.

Sometimes an idiom is responsible for a statement that doesn't stand up to literal reading. A follow-up story on a high-profile multiple birth reported that one of the quadruplets or octuplets or whatever they were "no longer requires oxygen." The meaning, of course, was that the infant no longer required *supplementary* oxygen, but we all need oxygen. (Thanks to my brother Terence for this example.)

COME OUT AND SAY IT

Writers sometimes tend to hint around at an idea rather than actually presenting it. That's fine in conversation, where a friendly listener nods as if to say "I know what you're getting at," but in writing it makes for statements so utterly unremarkable that they're not worth printing.

In a story about ABC's plans to challenge CNN in the 24-hour-news arena, it was pointed out that one of CNN's claims to fame was that it "broadcast the 1986 space shuttle explosion."

Uh, yes, and so did virtually every other TV network on the planet. The point was that CNN was the only major outlet broadcasting the Challenger launch *live* when the disaster occurred. Perhaps the reporter wasn't sure whether that was true, but if it wasn't, then what kind of claim to fame could there possibly be? And why would that sentence be worth writing? Heck, I'm sure CNN also broadcast JFK's assassination at one point or another via the Zapruder film, but it would be silly to point that out, now, wouldn't it?

ILLEGAL CLIPPING

Ride the D.C. area's Metro system and you'll hear the driver identify the train you're on by the station at the end of the line. Until recently, the Blue Line's end points were the Addison Road and Van Dorn Street stations. Only you never heard "Van Dorn Street"—it was always simply "Van Dorn." It was never simply "Addison"—Addison Road always got its "Road," but Van Dorn Street *never* got its "Street." (This might make some sense if Van Dorn Street were in a community known as "Van Dorn," but it isn't.)

Why am I boring you with Washington trivia? It's to examine yet another way in which people fail to say what they really mean: the curious phenomenon of linguistic laziness. If people were truly lazier than fecal matter, they would refer to the Addison Road stop as "Addison." But they don't. It's as if place names have a certain expected rhythm that's broken when a third word is added. I've seen the same thing with downtown Washington's Mount Vernon Square. Reporters writing about the area tend to lapse into *Mount Vernon* midway through the story. This is more dangerous than the Van Dorn example, because the D.C. area *does* have a Mount Vernon (George Washington's estate, a dozen or so miles down the Potomac in Virginia), and Mount Vernon Square ain't it.

For truly bizarre examples of this phenomenon, I think of a woman I once knew who clipped virtually everything she said, sometimes adding the not-quite-possessive, not-quite-plural *s* favored by Detroit autoworkers (who say things like "I used to work at Chryslers, but now I work at Fords!") and, oddly, the British (what *is* the deal with Reuter[s] and Slazenger[s]?). When she started talking about "Consumers," it took me a few moments to realize she meant the magazine Consumer Reports. When she said she read something in "USA," she was talking about USA Today.

WHEN SLANG IS
JUST PLAIN LAZY

Slang adds color to the language. It adds brevity as well, and in the process it sometimes even adds precision. *Fixer-upper* paints the picture much better, and faster, than *house sold with the understanding that it is in need of repairs.* So let me make this perfectly clear: I'm not always opposed to slang, just as I'm not necessarily opposed to wearing tennis shoes. It all depends on the occasion: You don't wear tennies to your grandma's funeral, and you don't use slang in newspaper stories about violent death.

A close cousin to slang is the phenomenon of permanent truncation, in which a term (*hashed browned potatoes*, for example) loses a few pounds (*hash browns*). I have no problem here, although reasonable editors will disagree over whether, say, *ice tea* has earned this status (this reasonable editor says it hasn't—that's *iced tea* to you).

Caught in the middle are those cute little truncations that have endeared themselves to the speaking and writing public with such brash persistence that everyone pretends to have forgotten these words' true identities:

Tux.
Limo.
Veggies.
Vegas.
Black and yellow Labs.

There are no tuxedos, limousines, vegetables or Labrador retrievers in Las Vegas, and indeed there *is* no Las Vegas. Well, OK, *Las Vegas* is still clinging to life in some circles. *Vegetables* is pretty far gone, though, and *limousine* and *tuxedo* are missing and presumed dead. Again, it's fine to use the truncated forms, even in writing, in the context of deliberate informality. But it's ridiculous to use these as actual words when writing with a straight face.

The genesis of this rant, by the way, was a late-night "infomercial" for one of those buttocks-strengthening devices.

The perky little host never, ever, referred to the body part in question as anything but "buns." Even in the most technical, explanatory parts of this "paid programming," it was buns this and buns that. Not exactly a truncation, but I think you can see how this set me off.

GIVING 110 PERCENT

Why You Needed Those
Math Classes After All

Word people are notorious for being poorly educated in matters of mathematics—"innumeracy," it's been called. Great writers who can figure percentage changes seem almost as rare as poetic mathematicians; it must be a right-brain-vs.-left-brain thing. I couldn't begin to tell you what a quadratic equation is, but I'll go over some common examples of innumeracy.

A Point on Percentages

If, say, the unemployment rate was 4 percent this year and 3 percent last year, how much did it fall? One percent? Wrong. It changed one *percentage point*, but one out of four is one-fourth, or 25 percent.

Less Than Zero?

I see this a lot: *The currency lost 300 percent of its value in the past year.* Or *Contributions to the fund fell fivefold.*
Uh-uh.
If the old number is 500 and the new number is 100, yes, the old number was five times as big. But that doesn't mean the decrease is 500 percent. Once something decreases 100 percent, it's *gone!* I've had much difficulty explaining this to people, but it's as simple as that. The answer is usually "Well, it was a *big* decrease!" Fine. Eighty percent, as in the preceding example, *is* a big decrease. You don't need to stretch the boundaries of modern mathematics to make that point. Increases can be 500 percent; decreases cannot. Case closed. Now get back to work, and be sure to give 110 percent.

When Numbers Get Meaningless

Too often reporters trying to use numbers hedge so much as to make those numbers utterly meaningless. I'm talking about sentences like this:

> *An average caseworker might handle up to 100 cases a month or more.*

OK, let's see: *up to* 100 cases a month, meaning it could be anything from zero to 100, but the upper limit is 100. But wait: "or more"! So the sentence says 100 is the most it could possibly be—but it could be more. And that's just the "average" caseworker. And it only "might" be true. In other words, the sentence says nothing; it just wastes valuable paper.

Once my head stops spinning, I try to get the writer to be more specific. If that fails, I usually change the sentence to something like this:

It's not unusual for a caseworker to handle 100 cases a month.

Not great (though I do like the sly Tom Jones reference), but it's safe and it conveys at least *some* information.

10 Times as Correct

Something might be 10 times as fast as or 20 times as big as something else, and that's the way to handle such expressions—not "10 times faster than." I suppose you could make the argument that "10 times faster" is acceptable, with the meaning being "11 times as fast," but I don't see why you'd bother. *Times* implies a comparison based on a multiplier, and a multiplier makes sense only in relation to the number it's multiplying. *As fast* preserves that relationship; *faster* does not. Boil the comparison down to its simplest form and you'll see that *twice as fast* makes a lot more sense than *one time faster*.

MATTERS OF
SENSITIVITY
Correctness, Political and Otherwise

The PC (personal computer) begat the tough questions I addressed in Chapter 3, and another PC (political correctness) figures prominently in this chapter. The language is continually evolving to steer around insensitivity in areas such as race, sex and sexual orientation. A publication that follows these changes too quickly can appear pandering or patronizing at best or like a leftist manifesto at worst. A publication that ignores such change can look quaint, dated or even extremely right-wing. Here I try to chart a sensible course.

"AFRICAN-AMERICAN" VS. "BLACK"

African-American is an appropriate term relating to the culture of black Americans (Kwanzaa and soul food are African-American), but it shouldn't be used interchangeably with *black* as a racial term.

For one thing, it's inaccurate. A white person from Johannesburg who moved to the United States and became a naturalized citizen would be an African-American. A black Caribbean native who moved to England would not. For better or worse, the intent of the term is to delineate the admittedly slippery concept of race, and so abandoning the term *black* makes it rather difficult to refer to the race of black people who don't happen to be American (assuming, of course, that such a person's race is somehow relevant). There is no racial difference between African-Americans and African-Canadians, so how can *African-American* constitute a race? I suppose you could refer to boxer Frank Bruno as an *African-Briton*, but that segues into my second point:

The term *African-American* avoids an important issue. In a perfect world we wouldn't need such labels, but racism, human nature (the differences between us are interesting to us—nobody objects to the term *blond*) and even sickle-cell anemia demand that anyone writing about real life be equipped with terms that refer to racial differences. There are those who will maintain that it's racist to use the word *black*, but isn't it worse to write something like *The Klan members admitted to the attack and said they did it because the victims were African-American*? Such a sentence lends undeserved dignity to the racists, as if they checked passports and genealogy before making the educated decision to harm a fellow human being. Racists don't do such things—they base their hatred purely on skin color, and this should never be forgotten.

"GAY" VS. "HOMOSEXUAL"

Yes, the appropriation of *gay* by homosexuals did rob us of a perfectly good synonym for *happy*. But the latter usage—and, frankly, this complaint—is getting rather tired. The new usage? It's here. It's queer. Get used to it.

Now then: Which is right, you ask, *gay* or *homosexual*? My answer is "both." And by that I mean both, not "either." In general, *homosexual* is the precise mechanical term, and *gay* is more accurate when referring to a lifestyle beyond the bedroom, just as *black* describes skin color and *African-American* describes certain cultural traditions. Unwavering consistency in using one term or the other tends to brand a publication as right-wing wacko (homosexual this and homosexual that) or left-wing freak (gay this and gay that). In stories long enough to do so, I prefer to establish a solid factual base with *homosexual* but use *gay* freely thereafter to avoid sounding clinical. Clinical publications (and, for that matter, left-wing and right-wing publications) are free to tailor this advice to their needs.

"GAY AND LESBIAN"

The phrase is well entrenched, but I can't help pointing out that speaking of *gays and lesbians* is analogous to saying *people and women*. Use *gay men and women* or *homosexual men and*

DIRTY MIND, CLEAN COPY

Why Every Copy Desk Could Use a
13-Year-Old Boy

A puerile sense of humor can be a big asset in the word business. I call it the Beavis and Butt-head factor. (Heh-heh—he said "big asset"!)

This means you should know why *Court Deals Blow to Homosexuals* is a bad headline. You should know why the previous sentence was *not* the place to abbreviate *headline*. You should know why *stiff* and *come* were to be avoided in Clinton impeachment stories.

These things can be subtle. In trying to think of a headline for a reporter's first-person account of the wonders of his Palm hand-held computer (they're no longer called *Palm Pilots*), my first idea was *A Man and His Palm: A Love Story*.

Heh-heh.

lesbians or even *gay men and lesbians* when such a phrase is appropriate.

"HE OR SHE," "HIM OR HER," "HIS OR HER," "HIS OR HERS"

It's unfortunate that the traditional all-purpose pronoun in these cases is the same as the male pronoun. Technically it's correct to write *Each person has his own standards* even when each person isn't a him, but that sounded dated and sexist even before the age of political correctness.

The "he or she" solution is fine if you're dealing with one or maybe two pronoun conflicts, but if it sends you down an endless road of "his or her" references, you might as well add a footnote apologizing to hermaphrodites.

The best solution—and it's almost always possible—is to recast problem sentences in the plural form:

 AWKWARD: *A trader can place his or her order by telephone or over the Internet.*

MUCH BETTER: *Traders can place their orders by telephone or over the Internet.*

Of course, this is a work-around and not a long-term reform of the language. Many writers in search of such reform like to alternate male and female pronouns. Others self-consciously choose female pronouns in a sort of grammatical affirmative action. Ask a sensible editor and she'll tell you these practices are silly.

Then how about enlisting *they*, *them*, *their* and *theirs* as honorary singular pronouns in the fight against sexist language? Well, maybe. Purists will be shocked, but I find this less objectionable than the other alternative solutions. Unless you were born in an ivory tower, you probably put plural pronouns to singular use in many a conversation (*"I went to Safeway yesterday—they have some great eggplants on sale!"*). For now it still seems illiterate in writing, but I think the oral precedent makes this solution to the sexist-language problem a leading contender for future honors. To review . . .

 GRAMMATICALLY CORRECT BUT SEXIST: *Every music lover has his own favorite album.*

GRAMMATICALLY AND POLITICALLY CORRECT BUT AWKWARD: *Every music lover has his or her own favorite album.*

POLITICALLY CORRECT BUT PATRONIZING: *Every music lover has her own favorite album.*

GRAMMATICALLY INCORRECT (FOR NOW) BUT INTUITIVELY PLAUSIBLE AND RATHER TEMPTING: *Every music lover has their own favorite album.*

IT'S OK TO BE A HYPHENATED AMERICAN

Use a hyphen in *African-American*, *Asian-American*, *Irish-American* and most other terms of dual ancestry or citizenship.

Latin American and *American Indian* are obvious exceptions; *French Canadian* is a not-so-obvious one but one that should be followed because of widespread usage. It means

"Canadian of French descent" only indirectly, referring most immediately to French-*speaking* Canadians. It has become politically correct in recent years to drop the hyphens in such terms, on the theory that the phrase *hyphenated Americans* is somehow an insult. If the hyphen is insulting, I suppose in 10 years the space between the words will be seen as blood libel and we'll end up writing *Italianamerican*. Stay tuned.

I'll Be Dammed

How much profanity should be allowed in print will vary widely among publications, so there's no way to prescribe one standard that would apply to both Hustler and the Ladies' Home Journal. But I would like to make one point on the subject: Misspelling a curse doesn't make it any less offensive. If *goddamn* and *son of a bitch* are offensive, so are *goddam* and *sonuvabitch*.

Physical Descriptions

It's ludicrous to give a physical description of a crime suspect and, in the name of political correctness, omit any reference to race. It could be argued that such descriptions are almost always useless anyway, but if you choose to print them they should be complete.

If you choose to give physical descriptions complete with race, keep in mind that precise terms should be used. As I argued earlier, black people are not necessarily African-American; they could be Canadian or British or Dutch or any other nationality.

HE SAID, SHE SAID

Quotations in the News

Just as a day without orange juice is like a day without sunshine, and apple pie without some cheese is like a kiss without a squeeze, a story without quotes is flat and lifeless. And you can quote me on that.

By the way, I've been accused of setting a bad example by using *quote* to mean "quotation." To which I reply, I may be a curmudgeon, but my age is well within double digits and I don't request extra starch at the laundry.

I use both terms in this book, but let me take my acceptance of the short form one step further: *Quote* is not only a perfectly acceptable shortening of *quotation*; it's a preferable term when describing those nuggets of speech that journalists mine from the living to give their stories credibility. When I hear *quotation*, I think of those nuggets of speech mined from the Bible and a host of dead people ("Anonymous" is one popular figure) and preserved for frequent repetition because of their pithiness. If someone in the newsroom yelled, "I have a quotation from Clinton," my reply might be "Is he quoting Thomas Jefferson or Abraham Lincoln?"

Here are some thoughts on the art of putting words in people's mouths.

INTRODUCING THE QUOTE

Full-sentence quotes should be introduced with commas. Multiple-sentence quotes should be introduced with colons. But this doesn't mean such punctuation should intervene every time quote marks are used. With partial quotes and titles of books, movies, plays, etc., punctuate the sentence as if the quotes weren't there:

 RIGHT: *He said, "I'm going outside."*

WRONG: *He said he was, "going outside."*

WRONG: *The play was titled, "Inherit the Wind."*

Still not convinced? Try this:

 WRONG: *He says things like, that.*

WRONG: *He says things like, "I'll kick your butt!"*

RIGHT: *He says things like that.*

RIGHT: *He says things like "I'll kick your butt!"*

Capitalization is another basic area in which full-sentence quotes and partial quotes differ. A conventionally introduced quote must begin with a capital letter:

He said, "It was a very good day."

But partial quotes—and full quotes that are fashioned to continue a thought already begun in the sentence—should not start with caps unless the first word is a proper noun.

Jones said it was "a very good day."
Despite the rain, Jones said, "it was a very good day."

The latter example is a tricky one. The *it* is lowercase because *Jones said* constitutes attribution for the whole sentence, not just the "good day" part. Jones is saying, essentially, "It was a good day despite the rain." If you capitalize *it* in the quote, you're saying that, despite the rain, Jones chose to speak the words "It was a very good day." The difference is subtle but important. Observe:

Though she didn't really like him, she said, "Let's do this again sometime."

In this sentence, *she said* is attribution for only the quoted matter. In the first part of the sentence, the writer is asserting a fact rather than paraphrasing the woman who's speaking. So *Let's* isn't lowercase, because it's not a continuation of the thought that began the sentence.

WHO SAYS "SAYS WHO"?

Generally, it's more straightforward and less pretentious to put *said* after the name of the speaker than to put it before— *Smith said*, not *said Smith*.

Note that I said "generally." This is one of those "whatever sounds better is fine" rules, but the following guidelines are almost always applicable.

Put *said* first when a descriptive element would otherwise come between the word and the speaker's name.

"Blah, blah, blah," said Smith, who is under psychiatric care.
"So what?" said Jones, 32.

If the *said* is embellished with a description of how or where the talking was done, keeping the word in its rightful place becomes vital:

 WORSE: *"I don't like to talk much," said Blow-hard yesterday in a telephone interview.*

BETTER: *"I don't like to talk much," Blowhard said yesterday in a telephone interview.*

In the "worse" construction, the "how" and "when" elements seem tossed in, in no particular order. The better example has a simple, straightforward narrative elegance.

WHEN THE ATTRIBUTION CAN GO

A quote that immediately follows an attributed quote (and is from the same person) can stand without attribution:

"I'm not going to stand for it," she said. "I just won't."

This liberty is often taken improperly to mean a quote that follows an attributed *paraphrase* can play by the same rules. The result is a just-hanging-there quotation, something that should be avoided.

 WRONG: *She said she was drawing the line at his drug use. "I'm not going to stand for it."*

RIGHT: *She said she was drawing the line at his drug use. "I'm not going to stand for it," she said.*

When the *said*s are getting just too numerous, a colon sometimes comes in handy to jury-rig a paragraph.

 ACCEPTABLE: *She said she was drawing the line at his drug use: "I'm not going to stand for it."*

WHERE THE ATTRIBUTION
SHOULD GO

A quote usually goes before its attribution, but there's at least one good exception: If a different person has just been quoted, it is of immense help to the reader to immediately make it clear that the person doing the talking is about to change.

 CONFUSING: *"Ali was like a god," one-time opponent George Foreman said. "He inspired me."*
"I think about him a lot," three-time opponent Ken Norton said.

BETTER: *"Ali was like a god," one-time opponent George Foreman said. "He inspired me."*
Three-time opponent Ken Norton said, "I think about him a lot."

Abbrevs. in Quotes

Should abbreviations be used in quotations? It's surprising how few stylebooks address this basic issue. My answer: Sometimes.

Some abbreviations are so much a part of the language that their spelled-out forms scarcely exist. *"Hey, mister! You'd better go see a doctor!"* is fine, but *"Hello, Doctor Smith, my name is Mister Jones"* looks a tad Elizabethan. At the other extreme, *"I'm Rep. Morris Udall from Tucson, Ariz."* conjures up a guy in a hurry who talks real funny.

With that in mind, use the following in quotes: *Dr.*, *Mr.*, *Mrs.*, *Jr.* and, obviously, *Ms.* (I reserve the right to add to this list when readers point out the other obvious candidates I forgot.)

Spell out other normally abbreviated words when they occur in quotations, including the following close calls:

> *Et cetera.*
> *Versus.*
> *Number* (as in *number one*, as opposed to *No. 1*).
> *The Reverend.*

Why *Dr.* but not *Rev.*? Well, people actually say "Rev." these days, usually sarcastically and often (at least in Washington, D.C.) in reference to Jesse Jackson or Sun Myung Moon. I'd be careful to avoid rendering someone's sincerely spoken "Reverend" in such a way that it could be construed as a dig.

And then there is the issue of military ranks. *Sgt.* doesn't look bad, but *Brig. Gen.* and especially *Spc.*, for "Specialist," do. And to have to write *Pfc.* when quoting someone saying "Private First Class" would be ridiculous.

Observe:

"Colonel Gray may think you're number one," Sgt. Vince Carter told Pfc. Gomer Pyle, "but if it comes down to him versus Corporal Boyle and me, I'm ready to call in the Reverend Billy Graham and Dr. Joyce Brothers to tell him you should be sent back to Mayberry, North Carolina. I'd call the Reverend Dr. Martin Luther King Jr. if he were still alive!"

CLARIFYING WITH BRACKETS

Brackets (or parentheses, depending on your style) in quotes are meant to help the reader, but they often become ugly and distracting. Here's one case where they could have been avoided:

ORIGINAL: *"Just look at the clout that Hispanics have . . . [Transportation Secretary] Federico Pena and [Secretary of Housing and Urban Development] Henry Cisneros," he said.*

BETTER: *"Just look at the clout that Hispanics have . . . Federico Pena and Henry Cisneros," he said. Pena is secretary of transportation, and Cisneros is secretary of housing and urban development.*

BETTER STILL: *"Just look at the clout that Hispanics have," he said, pointing to Federico Pena, the secretary of transportation, and Henry Cisneros, the secretary of housing and urban development.*

In the following case, the brackets just insult the reader's intelligence:

> *"There is a battle right now for [President] Clinton's soul,"* said a source aware of the policy division.

Uh-uh. Unless there is a chance *Clinton* could be mistaken for Hillary or Chelsea, an insertion like this, while correct in a very strict technical sense, is unwise. Bracketed material should be introduced into a quote only as a last resort, when clarification is desperately needed. Brackets are not the place for editors to demonstrate that they know more about grammar or style than the speaker—I've seen *"these days, less people are available"* changed to *"these days, [fewer] people are available,"* which is laughably pedantic.

Here are two examples, from the same rather dated story, of how awkward, unsightly bracketed material can and should be rearranged:

BEFORE: *"I thank [House Minority Whip Rep.] Newt [Gingrich] and the Republicans because they've given him another chance for a comeback,"* said Coelho.

AFTER: *"I thank Newt and the Republicans, because they've given him another chance for a comeback,"* Coelho said. Rep. Newt Gingrich, Georgia Republican, is the House minority whip.

BEFORE: *"We'd compromise where we had to. It comes down to where [House Speaker] Tom [Foley] and [House Majority Leader] Dick [Gephardt] get these votes,"* the official added.

AFTER: *"We'd compromise where we had to. It comes down to where Tom and Dick get these votes," the official added, referring to House Speaker Thomas S. Foley of Washington and House Majority Leader Richard A. Gephardt of Missouri.*

SINS OF OMISSION

Bracketed material should clarify language, not replace it—at least not without telltale ellipses.

WRONG: *"And then [Zivic] hit me below the belt," he said.*

It's unlikely the speaker said "And then hit me below the belt," but that's the implication of such a quote.

RIGHT: *"And then he [Zivic] hit me below the belt," he said.*

Sometimes such a deletion is necessary for taste reasons. The ellipsis rule still applies.

RIGHT BUT POSSIBLY OBJECTIONABLE: *"And then the bastard [Zivic] hit me below the belt," he said.*

WRONG: *"And then [Zivic] hit me below the belt," he said.*

RIGHT: *"And then . . . [Zivic] hit me below the belt," he said.*

Of course, I'm presenting an idealized guideline. In the real world, following such a rule might require a lot of late-night calls to reporters for a seemingly trivial detail ("Did he say 'he' in this spot where you clarify with brackets?"). Then again, perhaps one late-night call per reporter would be enough to make the rule clear.

He Said What?

What's wrong with the following sentence?

Major said talking with Sinn Fein would "turn his stomach."

Give up? Why would John Major talk about himself in the third person? It's likely he said "turn my stomach." (Now, Bob Dole might be another story.)

"Said, and Added"

Here's a principle that even good writers tend to violate, especially in fiction: You cannot splice a second clause onto a "he said" or "she said" type of attribution.

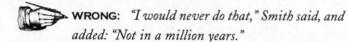 **WRONG:** *"I would never do that," Smith said, and added: "Not in a million years."*

WRONG: *"I'm leaving," Jones said, and walked out of the room.*

Why is this wrong? "I would never do that" is what Smith said, and the placement of *Smith said* indicates that. The first example, however, places *and added* in a parallel position; thus the *and added* clause is made dependent on the *Smith said* clause, which is already dependent on the quote. Smith didn't both *say* "I would never do that" and *add* "I would never do that," but the placement of the quotation at the beginning of the sentence suggests just that. For that construction to work at all, you'd need a sentence like this: *"I would never do that," Smith said and repeated under her breath.*

Beginning a sentence with a quote makes everything that follows dependent on that quote, unless the subject is changed or restated. *Smith* cannot logically do double duty as the subject of two clauses. If you want to use the same subject for more than one clause, consider using that subject to begin the sentence.

 RIGHT: *Smith said, "I would never do that," and added: "Not in a million years."*

RIGHT: *Jones said, "I'm leaving," and walked out of the room.*

Another option is to change the subject—or at least restate it.

 RIGHT: *"I would never do that," Smith said, and she added: "Not in a million years."*

RIGHT: *"I'm leaving," Jones said, and he walked out of the room.*

BEWARE OF RUN-ONS

Here's another often-ignored principle: When a partial quote
completes a thought, the quote should be closed as soon as
the thought is complete. Writers, especially news reporters,
tend to muck things up by taking the opportunity to tack on
extra quoted matter.

 WRONG: *He called the movie "fantastic. It was
one of the best films I've ever seen."*

Now, what did our hero call the movie? He called it fantastic. Period. He also called it one of the best films he had
ever seen. He did *not* call it fantastic-it-was-one-of-the-best-
films-I've-ever-seen.

 RIGHT: *He called the movie "fantastic."*
     *"It was one of the best films I've ever seen," he
said.*

Note the end-quote mark after "fantastic." That mark
should be deleted when a full quote continues into the next
paragraph, but this is a partial quote.

Another way to get around the run-on problem is to separate the salient partial quotes.

 RIGHT: *He called the movie "fantastic" and "one of
the best films I've ever seen."*

Another way to solve this problem is to move the
attribution.

"It Is I,"
Said the Fullback

Should editors "correct" quotes? No. Quotes are sacred.

This doesn't mean we need to reproduce every *um*, every *er*, every cough; it doesn't mean a reporter's transcription errors can't be corrected; and it certainly doesn't mean that stories should attempt to re-create dialect (plenty of literate people pronounce *should have* as "should of"). But it does mean that a reader should be able to watch a TV interview and read the same interview in the newspaper and not notice discrepancies in word choice.

Before radio and TV, let alone 24-hour cable news and C-SPAN, the lying journalist could rest assured that very few people would ever catch such deception. Today, however, it's

continued

pretty likely that somewhere someone is watching CNN and hearing "I ain't saying nothing to you [bleep]ing [bleep]ers" while reading a printed account of the same statement that says "I respectfully decline to comment, my good man." (OK, maybe I'm exaggerating, but you get the point.)

After all, what is the point of quote marks if not to signal that what's inside is a verbatim account of what was said?

It is often argued that quoting people accurately is somehow unfair, that reproducing the little flaws that everyone makes when speaking "makes them look stupid." Too bad. That's no reason to lie, which is what you're doing when you put quote marks around a non-quote.

Another problem with worrying about "making people look stupid" is that it introduces a troubling class calculus: If William Safire fails to use the subjunctive when he should have, you'll correct that, but will you do the same in a quote from a football player or a welfare mother? You have to decide on a "correct but not too correct" version of your stylebook to ensure that educated people don't look uneducated but uneducated people don't look too educated. Once you've gone this far, why not just make up all of your quotes?

A corollary to the class problem is the problem of cases where certain editors might *want* to make people look uneducated, or at least colorful. In a feature story on a Southern sheriff's down-home ways, do we want to impose the sequence of tenses on his yarn about a possum over yonder by the woodpile? Or how about this: If a big story were to break on a public official making a hilarious goof in a speech, wouldn't it be a little unfair to report this in a publication that essentially pretends nobody else in the world ever makes a grammatical mistake out loud?

I may sound strident on a lot of other points, but this is one where I truly believe that people who disagree with me are deranged. The answer is breathtakingly simple: It's our job to tell the *truth*.

WRONG: *The mutual fund is appropriate "for pretty much everybody, but we don't think anybody should put his entire nest egg in this product," McCall said.*

RIGHT: *The mutual fund is appropriate "for pretty much everybody," McCall said, "but we don't think anybody should put his entire nest egg in this product."*

You're the Editor

Just because someone says something, you don't have to print the quote, and the same rule applies to how much of a partial quote to use. Ideally, the stuff in quotes should be coherent even without the surrounding words.

Note these examples:

Previti said the "government found the situation very difficult."

This reads much better with the opening quotation marks moved over one word—keep *government*, but start the quote with *found*. You could even make an argument for keeping only *very difficult* within the quote marks, because that's the salient phrase.

The lawyer said the Tailhook convention held annually at the Las Vegas Hilton was the "Hilton's dirty little secret."

Same thing here. *Dirty little secret* is the quotable stuff—*Hilton's* works better as a non-quoted word (*hotel's* would be even better).

THE BIG TYPE

Headlines and Captions

The "display type" is all that many readers look at in many cases, and a misstep in 36 points, or under a photograph, is a lot more noticeable than one in the 9-point body type. Here are some things not to do.

SAY WHAT?

I declare this "World Syntax Day."
I proclaim this "World Syntax Day."
I label this "World Syntax Day."
I pronounce this "World Syntax Day."
I say this "World Syntax Day."

Wait a minute! I *say* it World Syntax Day? *Say* doesn't work the same way as the other words, does it?

This isn't an error you're likely to find in a story, but it happens regularly in headlines. The omission of "to be" verbs and "helping" verbs is a standard headline practice (*3 Killed in Shootout* is fine; it needn't be *3 Are Killed in Shootout*), but headlinese has its limits. You can omit these kinds of verbs only in a headline's *main* verb. Attach *Police Say* to the beginning of this headline and *to say* becomes the main verb; therefore you should not write *Police Say 3 Killed in Shootout*. The active nature of the verb *to kill* adds an element of ambiguity to this headline; you could ask "Three killed whom?" *Police Say 3 Were Killed in Shootout* is one solution. You could also say *3 Killed in Shootout, Police Say* (*killed* becomes the main verb) or *Police Say 3 Died in Shootout* (*died* does not require a helping verb).

The stylebook of my employer, the Washington Post, contains a nice entry on this rule, but even the Post doesn't always follow it. For example, under the perfectly acceptable headline *4 Americans Shot Dead in Pakistan* was the secondary head *Oil Company Workers Gunned Down 2 Days After Kasi Convicted*. After Kasi convicted *whom*? You cannot assume the reader will fill in the *was* or *is* for anything but the main verb. Possible alternatives in this case: *Oil Company Workers Killed 2 Days After Kasi Was Convicted* or *Oil Company Workers Gunned Down 2 Days After Kasi Conviction*.

"Ask" and "Seek" in Headlines

In a headline-count emergency, *ask* is permissible as a substitute for *seek* (*Clinton Asks Probe of Incident*), but *seek* is vastly preferable. *Asks for*, of course, would be fine, but *asks* alone is grating.

"Seen" vs. "Seen as" in Headlines

Traditionalists often wince when they see *seen* in headlines, but it should be pointed out that *seen as* is perfectly fine (*Clinton Seen as Likely Winner*). Personally, I think it's rather elegant, if any shortcut can be seen as such. Now, *seen* alone is a different story. *Clinton Seen Likely Winner*, or any head using *seen* that way, would never win my approval. The *as* is indispensable.

Headlines and Tense

While most headlines should be in the present tense, the past tense is necessary in stories reporting a new disclosure of an old (even day-old) event. A story about the search of Vince Foster's office after his suicide was a good example—*Clinton Aides Searched Office*, not *Clinton Aides Search Office*.

Relationships

An agreement, disagreement or other relationship between two people or two entities is signified by a hyphen, not a comma. It seems like a simple point, but it's one of the most common errors in newspapers today. Nobody (I hope) would write *the Ali, Frazier fight*, but plenty of people write (especially in headlines) *Conrail, CSX merger* or *U.S., China pacts*.

Wrong. Repeat after me: Ali-Frazier fight, Conrail-CSX merger, U.S.-China pacts.

U.S., China pacts would mean "both U.S. pacts and China pacts." *U.S.-China pacts* means "pacts between the United States and China."

BAD GESTURES: CAPTIONS AND CLICHES

> *In happier times, they share a meal, unaware of the struggle ahead.*

The caption cliche *in happier times* is useful (like many cliches), but it's best to write around it. As for *unaware of the struggle ahead*, well, it just isn't newsworthy that people are unable to predict the future.

> *Fed Chairman Alan Greenspan addresses senators as Vice Chairman Alice Rivlin looks on.*

I'll admit that *looks on* is awfully useful when you have to identify a subject who isn't really doing much of anything. But I prefer just plain boring to boring and cliched. How about:

> *Fed Chairman Alan Greenspan addresses senators. At right is Vice Chairman Alice Rivlin.*

Another quirk of caption writers is their fondness for the word *chat.* Two people never seem to talk to each other in a cutline; they always "chat." If you can verify that the pictured members of the Joint Chiefs of Staff were engaged in the kind of mindless small talk that neighbors exchange over a back-yard fence, by all means use *chat.* If you don't know what they were saying, though, *talk* is the word.

Perhaps the worst caption cliche of all, though, is the routine use of the word *gesture*. If the existence of a gesture is obvious enough for the caption writer to notice it, the reader doesn't need to be told about it. Notice that I said *routine* use: There's nothing wrong with pointing out a gesture if such an explanation would add to the reader's understanding:

As Don Vito Corleone in "The Godfather," Marlon Brando makes the Mafia gesture for "you die tomorrow."

9

DASH IT ALL, PERIOD
The Finer Points of Punctuation

As the chapter title suggests, this is in no way a complete overview of punctuation. But I hope you enjoy my pot shots.

NO WAY, JOSE

It's not that I'm dead set against accent marks. If your publication has the time and resources to use accents and other diacritical marks correctly, go for it. But I maintain that it's impossible to use them consistently and correctly in a deadline-intensive medium such as daily newspaper journalism. If you can't use them consistently and correctly, you shouldn't use them at all.

Meet Renee. Or is it Renée? If this is a name you've obtained from a wire-service story, from public records, or indeed from any source that might not have the inclination (or, as in the wire services' case, the technology) to preserve that tiny little French import, you can find out only by asking Renee herself. And the truth is, you can't always ask Renee. Renee might not even be alive.

So it's fine and dandy if you find out that the Renee your reporter interviewed likes the accent mark, but if you use it, you'll be using it alongside plenty of other names that should have one but don't.

You could make an argument for including accent marks in words other than names—*resume* when it means "curriculum vitae," for example, or *pate* when it doesn't mean the top of someone's head—but I prefer to stay consistent and simply maintain that English is a language without accent marks, even when it's borrowing words from languages that do have them.

KNOW YOUR S FROM A HOLE
IN THE GROUND

Proper nouns ending in the letter *s* tend to sprout apostrophes whether they're needed or not.

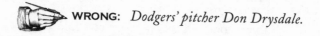 **WRONG:** *Dodgers' pitcher Don Drysdale.*

WRONG: *Monkees' singer Davy Jones.*

Usages such as these are simply labels (*Dodgers pitcher, Monkees singer*); they're not possessives. When in doubt, substitute an equivalent word that doesn't end in *s* and see if it would sound better as a possessive: Would you say *team's pitcher Don Drysdale* or *team pitcher Don Drysdale*? The latter, right? So it's *Dodgers pitcher Don Drysdale*. Would you say *band's singer Davy Jones*? No—it would be *band singer*, just as it would be *Monkees singer*. There are, of course, plenty of legitimate possessive constructions:

 RIGHT: *The Monkees' singer, Davy Jones* (the band's singer).

RIGHT: *The Dodgers' pitcher, Don Drysdale* (the team's pitcher).

Possessives With S's

Most newspapers use an apostrophe alone—*Connors' forehand* and not *Connors's forehand*. I disagree, and I'm happy to be working for a newspaper that feels the same way I do. The same rules should apply across the alphabet, and I fear that this exception is what causes the dreaded "Burt Reynold's" problem. If someone's name is *Reynolds*, the possessive is either *Reynolds'* or *Reynolds's*.

Plurals, of course, are an exception. So you would write *the United Nations' silly acronyms* and even *the Red Sox' schedule*.

POSSESSIVES WITH Z'S AND X'S

It's *Sanchez's*, not *Sanchez'*; *Phoenix's*, not *Phoenix'*. As I just pointed out, though, you'd make an exception for a creative plural such as *Red Sox*.

DESCRIPTIVE VS. POSSESSIVE

Use no hyphen and no apostrophe in constructions such as *seven months pregnant*. It's descriptive, not possessive or modifying.

On the other hand, *two years* is possessive in *two years' probation*, so the apostrophe is needed.

BULLET MAGIC

The most common problem with bulleted lists is an absence of parallel construction. If the first bulleted item is a declarative sentence in the present tense, the rest should also be declarative sentences in the present tense. Each item must be a continuation of the introductory sentence (note how the following bulleted items do just that).

The following is purely a matter of style, but I prefer to see bulleted items that:

- Are introduced with a colon.
- Begin with a capital letter and end with a period (not a semicolon), even if they aren't complete sentences.
- Eschew the annoying *and* that list makers of the semicolon school like to insert after the penultimate item.

Colon Surgery

Don't break up a perfectly good sentence with a colon just because a number of items are about to be listed. Lists need to be preceded with colons only when they are introduced abruptly, with no introduction, or with *the following* or *as follows* or *here are* or something like that. Don't use the colon after *the problems include* or *the members of the task force are.*

Subtitles

Use a colon between a book's title and its subtitle:

> *Richard Durham co-wrote Muhammad Ali's autobiography, "The Greatest: My Own Story."*

Commas

Commas don't seem to inspire shouting matches the way hyphens do, but opinions on their proper use probably vary even more widely. Because the comma often serves to symbolize a pause in speech, its use is subject to the vagaries of the human ear. There are hard-and-fast rules about commas, of course, but within those rules there is plenty of room for nuance and interpretation. The following items address common comma problems.

"And" and "But"

How do you know whether to use a comma when these conjunctions link two clauses?

If there's a new subject—or the old subject is restated—use the comma. If the second clause shares a subject with the first (and that subject is not restated), don't use the comma. Here's the kind of mistake I often see:

Mike looked in the boys' room, but didn't find anything.

Wrong. This is a run-on sentence starring two actors: *Mike* and *But*. Drop the comma to avoid divorcing the second half of the sentence from *Mike*.

 RIGHT: *Mike looked in the boys' room but didn't find anything.* (Just one subject; no comma.)

RIGHT: *Mike looked in the boys' room, but he didn't find anything.* (*He* is a restatement of the subject; comma.)

RIGHT: *Mike looked in the boys' room, but Carol didn't.* (New subject; comma.)

Of course, there are always exceptions. When what comes after the *but* is an aside, a little adjunct that really has no subject, the comma is appropriate.

 RIGHT: *Mike kept looking, but not for long.*

And when *and* is in a causal relationship with the rest of the sentence, the comma should be omitted:

Turn the corner and you'll find a row of charming antique shops.

COMMA WHEN, COMMA WHERE

Unless the comma cartel imposes an embargo, the usual rules apply. People seem eager to omit commas in sentences like the following:

> *They arrived at 1313 Mockingbird Lane where Lily and Herman Munster live.*

As opposed to the 1313 Mockingbird Lane where the Munsters don't live? You need a comma before *where*.

> *Potsie Weber tried to pal around with the Fonz who told him to "sit on it."*

Same principle. Add the comma. It's clear in both cases, as in most such sentences, that there's a positive ID of the proper noun involved. The no-comma approach should be used only when that is in question:

> *Is that the Archie who married Edith or the Archie who hangs out with Jughead?*

HER ONLY FRIEND? JUST ONE OF HIS MANY WIVES?

Let's assume for the sake of argument that Nicole Brown Simpson had more than one friend. Therefore, don't use a comma between *her friend* and *Ronald Lyle Goldman*. Along the same lines (though this point is subjective, not grammatical), the phrase *Nicole Brown Simpson and her friend* has the same sort of finality about it, as though she had no other friends. I prefer to say *Nicole Brown Simpson and a friend of hers* unless space is at a premium.

The same logic dictates that *John Smith and his wife Mary* implies he's a bigamist. If there's only one friend, wife, sister, brother or whatever, the comma is needed. If there are more than one, the comma is wrong.

"Jr." and "Inc.," Not "Comma-Jr." and "Comma-Inc."

Don't use a comma before *Jr.* or *Inc.*, regardless of the person's or company's preference.

This is an AP rule, so other style manuals may differ, but AP's logic (found also in "The Elements of Style") is persuasive: The terms are inherently restrictive (Desi Arnaz and Desi Arnaz Jr. are two different people, right?). Also, introducing the "before" comma means you also have to introduce an "after" comma if a *Jr.* or *Inc.* occurs midsentence, which would become awkward.

A Comma, Because

Many arbiters of usage insist that *because* should never be preceded by a comma, but I disagree. Negative constructions in particular often need the comma to clarify which part of the sentence *because* modifies. Observe the difference between the following examples:

> *She didn't wear her raincoat, because it was too warm.*

> *She didn't wear her raincoat because it was raining; she wore it because it matched her outfit.*

Once again, we have a distinction between an essential clause and a nonessential clause. In the first example, you can drop the clause and the sentence is still true. In the second example, the sentence's meaning depends on the clause.

Of Course, of Course

There are two kinds of *of courses*, one that takes a comma and one that doesn't. With the comma, it's a "matter of fact" or "by the way" sort of interjection:

> *Yes, I can make it Friday. Of course, I'll have to cancel my other appointments.*

Without the comma, it's much more emphatic:

> *Will I be there? Of course I will.*

Helpful hint: If the word *course* is stressed enough that you could put it in italics, delete the comma.

Hi, Comma

"Hi Bill!" This is fine in an e-mail message, but in actual writing a comma is needed after the *hi* or whatever remark you're directing to the person whom you then name.

If the on-line world is any indication, this simple convention is known by very, very few people. Chat transcripts are full of phrases like *Good point Al* and *Nice going Cindy*. My favorite example is from a chat between a starlet named Alicia and her fawning male fans. At the end of the session someone typed *Thanks for coming by Alicia*. If you don't see the problem with that, you don't have the dirty mind that every good copy editor needs.

NO THANKS TO YOU

Same principle as the preceding item. *No thanks* means just that: As far as thanks go, there are none.

The polite addition of *thanks* or *thank you* after a negative response requires a comma:

> *"Would you like a martini?"*
> *"No, thanks."*

MY POINT IS, USE THE COMMA

What I'm saying is, use a comma to set off the introductory clause in sentences like this one. You could argue that there's no grammatical reason to do so, but I think it would be pedantic to deny the pause that occurs naturally in this popular way of speaking (and writing).

HOMETOWNS

AP style stipulates that no comma be used when a hometown (or home country or home state or company, etc.) is set off with *of*:

> *Bob Hartley of Chicago and Gabe Kotter of Brooklyn, N.Y., attended the event.*

The stylebook does not address what to do when a hometown is introduced on a second reference, but as every right-thinking editor knows, the issue becomes one of essential clause vs. nonessential clause. On a second reference, we've already been introduced to the person in question, and thus that person's hometown is not a defining factor. Thus the comma is necessary:

> *Bob Hartley and Gabe Kotter attended the event. Hartley, of*
> *Chicago, passed along greetings from his friend Jerry Robin-*
> *son, who couldn't make it.*

Aside from the sound grammatical reason, *Hartley of Chicago* has an awfully medieval sound to it, like *Theodoric of York*.

Serial Commas

Newspapers, by and large, don't use 'em. Other publications usually do. So it would be *red, white and blue* in the Washington Post but *red, white, and blue* in your doctoral thesis.

But what a lot of newspaper editors don't know is that the serial comma is sometimes necessary even in newspaper style—it should be used if any item in a series already contains the word *and* (or *or*, as the case may be):

> *His favorite comedy teams were Laurel and Hardy, Abbott*
> *and Costello, and Bob and David.*

Devotees of the AP stylebook know this as the "toast, juice, and ham and eggs" rule.

Also use a serial comma if the items are awkwardly long or if each item—whatever the length—would stand as a complete sentence:

> *I like Trix, I like Lucky Charms, and I like Cocoa Pebbles.*

Ellipses

Ellipses are used to indicate the omission of words and sometimes to create a trailing-off effect at the end of a sentence.

They consist of three dots separated by "thin" spaces (see below) and surrounded by spaces:

> *"I don't remember . . . what happened," she said.*

Those three dots may or may not be preceded by a period, depending on whether the omission is in the middle of a sentence. (Note that I'm speaking of a period plus ellipses: There is no such thing as a *four-dot ellipsis*.) The period, as always, is flush with the preceding letter, and there is a space (a real space, not a thin space) between the period and the first ellipsis:

> *"This is a fine mess. . . . Why don't you do something about it?"*

. . . AND ANOTHER THING . . .

There is no need to use ellipses at the beginning or end of a quote, except perhaps to create the feeling of a trailing-off at the end (*I thought I did the right thing, but then again . . .*). It's silly to indicate omission at the beginning or end of a quote, since virtually all quotes are from people who have spoken before in their lives and will do so again.

TOO RICH, TOO THIN

To avoid a line break that might split up the dots, two *thin spaces* are usually used in place of space-bar spaces:

> .[thin].[thin].

While the term *thin space* is nearly universal in the newspaper world, word-processing programs might use other terms, such as *non-breaking space, mandatory space* or *hard space*. In HTML, it's a *non-breaking space*.

It's a common misconception among editors seeking a typographical nuance that thin spaces are thinner than ordinary spaces. They aren't, at least inherently, although they often *end up* that way. Here's the scoop: The thin space is the narrowest space between words that is allowed by a system's typesetting specifications. The reason it can end up thinner than other spaces is that it *stays* that width no matter how much the regular old spaces on the same line expand in the justification process. So thin spaces will look the same as other spaces in ragged type (where they still might be needed to avoid unwanted end-of-line splits) and in headlines (where they never make any difference). In headlines, in fact, I prefer, like many publications, to omit the spaces between ellipses entirely (but the spaces before and after must be retained).

Thin spaces are also used to separate single quote marks and double quote marks when there's a quote within a quote (see Page 94).

HYPHENS

Ah, the hyphen. When I was young and doctrinaire (yes, now I'm mellow, damn it!), this was my favored battlefield. Compound modifiers must be hyphenated, I insisted, and essentially I still believe this. Still, an awful lot of people believe the hyphen is intrinsically intrusive. I often think those who hate hyphens don't understand hyphens, but a lot of people in this camp have rather impressive credentials. For my feelings on the hyphenation of compound modifiers, see Chapter 2.

THE "OTHER" DASH

In the world of hoity-toity publishing (scholarly papers, books and some magazines), a little critter called the *en dash* is used with numerals (*The Wildcats clinched the 1983–84 championship with a 10–1 record*) and, more important for this discussion, as a stand-in for multiple hyphens in longer-than-two-word modifiers. The en is roughly the size of a capital *N*—wider than the hyphen but narrower than the regular (*em*) dash, and I suppose the theory is that the extra length allows it to reach back and connect words that didn't get connected in the first place (*high school–age students, 1.1 million–member union*). It doesn't work for me, and I'm sure it doesn't work for the 98 percent of the population for whom an en dash might as well be a track-and-field event. When you create a visual link between two words, it has the side effect of divorcing those words that are not so linked. So to me it's easier to read the indisputably incorrect *high school age students* than the allegedly hypercorrect *high school–age students*, which strongly links *school* and *age* but leaves the intimately related word *high* high and dry. Advocates of the en also use it where I would use a single hyphen in phrases such as *New York-based corporations*; there, however, the capitalization of *New York* provides a visual link that makes a second hyphen unnecessary.

I will admit to some innocent experimentation with this punctuation mark in college, but I didn't en-hale. This youthful indiscretion came in cases where an intrinsic hyphen (as in a hyphenated proper noun) was part of a modifier that also required an editorially generated hyphen. It seemed to me that phrases such as *the Kubler-Ross-espoused theory* and *the Sanchez-Vicario-led Spanish team* required a second-level hyphen, an uber-hyphen of sorts. But I got over it. The added visual nicety of an en dash in such cases was overridden by a populist streak that raised the question "If you're going to deem this punctuation mark *correct*, shouldn't it at least *exist* on the typewriter keyboard?" That was in the early 1980s, when people still used typewriters, but the question remains relevant today. The software makers (shame on them) require some contortions to produce a true em or en dash, but it's as easy as ever to type a hyphen or two, and I think the hyphen and the "normal" (two-hyphen) dash are the choices that those of us who aren't English professors should stick to.

LINE BREAKS

Keep your dictionary handy if your computer system forces you to think about such things, because the obvious answer is often wrong. *Acknowledgment* breaks after the syllable *knowl*, not after *know*, for example. Don't ever forget that syllables are key—thus, *trust-ed* is a fine break (at least for newspapers, though publications with wider columns often forbid breaking off a mere two letters) but *crush-ed* is decidedly not OK. And remember that when *th* or *ch* or any other letter combination forms a single sound, those letters must be kept together: Break *Buchanan* as *Bu-chan-an*, not *Buc-han-an*.

Words that are spelled the same but pronounced differently (*heteronyms*, or *non-homophonic homographs* if you prefer) present another problem. Take the word *present*: The way I used it in the previous sentence, it would be hyphenated as *pre-sent*. In *present and accounted for*, however, it would be *pres-ent*.

Finally, when tinkering with end-of-line hyphens, beware of a choice that would mislead the reader. For example, when *reinvent* breaks at the end of a line, it's better to go with *re-invent* than *rein-vent*, to avoid presenting the reader with the one-syllable word *rein*.

The results of a valid but misleading line break can be humorous. The front page of the March 18, 1999, New York Times carried a story about "johns" in San Francisco who were sent to a little class about the horrors of prostitution. In at least one edition, readers found this sentence, presented thusly:

> *Of the 2,181 men who have taken the class since it began four years ago, only 18 have been rear-rested and prosecuted after their names were checked against the program's list of participants.*

Rear-rested! The rest of the men kept their rears busy, I suppose.

ADVERBS AND OTHER "-LY" WORDS

Hyphens should not be used to link adverbs to the words they modify, even when the two words make up a compound modifier. *An easily led group*, for example, is correct—no hyphen.

But beware: Not all words that end in *ly* are adverbs. I've seen people refuse to hyphenate *family-run businesses*, citing the "-ly rule." This is an extreme example; more likely to cause confusion are adjectives ending in the suffix *ly*, such as *friendly*, *masterly* and *manly*. Remember that with adverbs, [*blank*]*ly* means "in a [blank] manner." Apply that test to the preceding examples and you get nonsense ("in a friend manner," "in a master manner," "in a man manner"). *Family*, of course, does not mean "in a fami manner."

This no-hyphen rule should also be suspended when multiple hyphens are necessary: *a not-so-logically-consistent position*.

Fools' Compounds

Occasionally a modifier will look for all the world like a compound one, drawing the hyphen the way a cagey basketball player draws a foul in the closing seconds of a close game. The Arizona Republic, bless its heart, hyphenated compound modifiers religiously when I was in high school, and occasionally it would print *color-TV sets* or a similar clunker. A color TV set isn't a set of color TV, it's a TV set that is color. *Color* modifies *set*, so the hyphen is wrong. Here's one that's even trickier: *grilled cheese sandwich*. At first glance the term looks wrong without a hyphen, but think about it: The *sandwich* is what's grilled, not the cheese. Finally, one for the right-wing-conspiracy-nut community: *one world government*. I've seen it written as *one-world government*, which works in a way, but the term's basic meaning is not so much "a government that treats the world as one" as it is "a single government for the world."

Straight Talk

Don't use a hyphen in phrases such as *third straight victory*.

Yes, I've heard the argument that the victories may or may not have been "straight." True enough, but how does that turn *third straight* into a compound modifier? *Straight* is being used as a synonym for *consecutive* in such a case, and I have no problem with that. If you do have a problem with it, fine. Use *consecutive*. But don't use the hyphen.

BAD HAIR DAY

Those who know me as a hyphenation stalwart will be surprised to learn that I oppose the hyphen in this case. *Bad-hair day*, as in *day of bad hair*, certainly makes sense, but I don't think that's the way the phrase is truly meant to be read. It's *bad hair day*, as in . . .

> *"What kind of hair day are you having?"*
> *"I'm having a bad hair day."*

See what I mean? "I'm having a bad hair day" isn't an answer to the question "What kind of day are you having?"—it's an answer to the question "What kind of hair day are you having?" In other words, as far as this expression goes, every day is a hair day, whether good, bad or indifferent. Think of *bad tennis day*, as in a day when rain prevents serving 'em up.

PARENTHESES: 1) DON'T DO THIS

The increasingly popular single parenthesis is not a legitimate punctuation mark. Numbers or letters in numbered or lettered lists should be followed by periods, like so:

1. *One.*
2. *Two.*
3. *Three.*

If such a device is necessary in midsentence, use full parentheses, like so:

> *She likes her copy-editing job because (a) the lack of a lunch break discourages overeating, (b) the salary discourages friv-*

olous spending on material goods and (c) the crusty old men she is forced to work with make messy office romances a non-issue.

ONE SPACE AFTER PERIODS

Yes, we old-timers all learned in typing class that you put two spaces after a period, exclamation point, question mark or colon. Well, unlearn that—unless you're still using a typewriter.

Professionally typeset copy—and these days that includes even that Microsoft Works document you created on your Packard Bell bare-bones Pentium and spit out through a Hewlett-Packard inkjet—doesn't use the typewriter convention.

QUESTIONS GET QUESTION MARKS

Found when slotting a column one evening during my Washington Times days:

"Did you read the headlines this morning in the Washington Times," he announced on the House floor.

"Do you think this is correct," the copy chief declared.

QUESTIONS THAT AREN'T

Sentences that contain a question should end in question marks, but those that only imply a question should not.

WRONG: *The larger question is whether the casino gambling should be allowed in Prince George's County or elsewhere in Maryland?*

"I Wonder . . ." and "Guess What" Are Not Questions

Use no question mark after a statement like *I wonder if it's going to rain today*. There's an implied question within, sure, but the speaker is stating that he wonders about something, not asking whether he does.

Similarly, though a questioning tone of voice is used when a person says "Guess what," that is also not a question. It's an imperative sentence, a command that the other person should guess.

"Bob"? How Wacky!

Avoid identifying people as *Lawrence "Larry" Horn* or *Robert "Bob" Smith*. Pick *Lawrence* or *Larry*, *Robert* or *Bob*. Let the full reference stand with quotes on a nickname that's not just a diminutive (*Carmine "The Big Ragoo" Ragusa*) or one that bears no relation to the real name (*William "Scott" Jones*).

Speaking of nicknames, when one is used without the person's real name, omit the quote marks:

Carlos the Jackal, but *Illich "Carlos the Jackal" Ramirez.*
Tip O'Neill, but *Thomas P. "Tip" O'Neill.*
Magic Johnson, but *Earvin "Magic" Johnson.*

ANIMALS AND CHARACTERS

The names of animals and fictional characters do not take quotation marks. It's *Fido* and *Howard Borden*, not *"Fido"* and *"Howard Borden."*

SEMICOLONS

The semicolon is an ugly bastard, and thus I tend to avoid it. Its utility in patching together two closely related sentences is to be admired, but patches like that should be a make-do solution, to be used when nothing better comes to mind. So I don't really have much to say about this punctuation mark, other than to offer a protocol for when it should kick in as a "supercomma" of sorts to separate items in a series—and to lobby against the ill-advised AP practice (which, curiously, is not codified in the AP stylebook) of using a serial *comma*, and not a serial semicolon, in a series that's otherwise dependent on semicolons. If you have to go with the semicolon, you should stick with it to the end.

Use semicolons if an item in the series contains a comma:

I got up; had toast, juice and milk; and brushed my teeth.

Exception: Commas alone present no confusion in series where ages are the only intervening element:

John Smith, 36, Mary Jones, 24, and Bob White, 22.

Use the semicolon when two intimately related sentences are fused together without the word *and*:

I looked outside; the weather was not nice.

Follow the usual rules in series introduced by colons, a situation where many editors insist on semicolons.

Four players were listed among the century's greatest athletes: Sampras, McEnroe, Borg and Laver.

SLASHES

The slash (/), or virgule, is a punctuation mark of last resort. It should be left in proper names and trademarks, if it's clear that that's what was intended, but in most other cases it can be replaced by a hyphen or a perfectly good English word such as *on* or *of* or *for*. A corporate title such as *vice president/sales* should be recast as *vice president for sales*.

And/or, however, should get the slash in the rare case that it can't be replaced by something more elegant (see Page 101).

QUOTATION MARKS WITH
OTHER PUNCTUATION

Commas, like periods, always go inside quote marks:

"I wrote 'The Sun Also Rises,' " Hemingway said.

Semicolons and colons never go inside quote marks:

He never watched "Cheers"; he didn't think it was all that funny.

Quotes ending in question marks should not routinely take a comma, either inside or outside:

"What's wrong with you?" she asked.

Sometimes, however, the juxtaposition of a question mark and a comma is inevitable:

The actress, who had a bit part in the film version of "Who's Afraid of Virginia Woolf?," died Monday at age 97.

Question marks and exclamation points can go either inside or outside, depending on the meaning:

"What about 'Seinfeld'?" he asked.

His response to everything was "Huh?"

Can anybody really sing "The Star-Spangled Banner"?

In American English, commas and periods go inside quote marks, period. Even single quotes.

 RIGHT: *"I saw 'Damn Yankees,'" he said.*

WRONG: *"I saw 'Damn Yankees',"he said.*

SPEAKING OF SINGLE QUOTES

In American English, single quotation marks have only two roles: One, they're used when a quotation occurs within another quotation; two, they're used in newspapers, as a matter of typographical style, in headlines and other headings.

Some writers seem to think "minor" quoted matter, such as nicknames, is not worthy of the full quote treatment and thus gets single quotes, but they are mistaken.

SINGLE AND DOUBLE QUOTES
A Common Error

Wire copy that contains quotes within quotes tends to arrive
screwed up: Instead of a single end-quote before a double end-
quote, you'll see a double end-quote before a single end-quote.
Why? The wire services' standard set of characters doesn't
contain a double quote mark. Instead, double quotes are made
by combining two single quotes. Your newspaper's computer
system (or at least every newspaper computer system I've
used) is smart enough to "read" a consecutive pair of single
quotes as a double quote, but it's not smart enough to know
that a consecutive *trio* of single quotes is another thing altogether. So it pairs off the first two quote marks it sees, leaving the third one hanging. Smart editors know to be on the
lookout for this—and to insert a thin space between single
and double quote marks.

THE CURMUDGEON'S STYLEBOOK

Details, Details

And now for the main event: the stylebook portion of this stylebook. Here you'll find a catalog of the many things that can go wrong in print—commonly repeated misconceptions as well as usage errors. If you're looking for a specific topic, the index is the best place to start.

A, AN Pronunciation, not spelling, rules. Vowel sounds get the *an*; consonant sounds get the *a*. Note, however, that a vowel doesn't necessarily produce a vowel sound. *Uniform*, for example, is pronounced "YOO-ni-form," and thus it does not merit an *an*.

The biggest source of controversy on this issue is, for some reason, *a historic*. Some British people pronounce *historic* as "istoric," and that has led many Americans to believe *an historic* is correct. It is not.

Many Americans will argue that they say "an istoric"— that may be true, but it's because they're letting *an* do the driving. Ask them to pronounce *historic* all by itself and you'll no doubt hear the *h*.

ABOUT, SOME Don't make a definite number sound like a wild guess to avoid writing out a number at the beginning of a sentence, as in *Some 44 people were killed*. Either you know it's 44 or you don't. If you know, it's *Forty-four people were killed*. If you don't, it's *About 45 people were killed*. *Some* is a wimpy cross between *about* and *I know*; *about* works only with nice, round numbers.

AN ACCIDENT WORKING This phrase is a favorite of radio traffic reporters. It means, of course, that police are working at an accident scene, and it's a phrase parroted directly from the police. Even worse, the reporters sometimes say "*We* have an accident working," parroting even the cops' personal pronoun.

ADIDAS In addition to the capitalization issue discussed in Chapter 3 (the logo says *adidas*, but proper nouns must be capitalized), this brand of athletic shoes presents a singular-plural problem. *He wore his Adidas* is commonly used in the plural sense, the same way you might say *She wore her Nikes*. But the *s* in *Adidas* is not a plural marker; it's part of the name. To avoid the hopelessly clumsy *He wore his Adidases*, make the trademark an adjective and find yourself a noun, as in *He wore his Adidas shoes*.

ADJECTIVE PILEUPS It's nice to be concise, but too many writers and editors take the idea to extremes by piling multiple adjectives—and, worse, nouns-turned-adjectives—in front of their nouns until the actual point of a sentence is as delayed as the Muhammad Ali fights used to be on ABC's "Wide World of Sports." This trend is exacerbated by the freedom from hyphens that many editors (not I!) encourage. If editors added all the hyphens their adjective-piling ways made necessary, they'd quickly see why most of these modifiers should be framed with a few extra words and moved to the back of the sentence. The following example, which you might recognize from earlier in the book, is a relatively tame one.

 WRONG: *Capital gains tax cut bill opponents held a news conference yesterday.*

TECHNICALLY RIGHT: *Capital-gains-tax-cut-bill opponents held a news conference yesterday.*

THE PURIST'S SOLUTION: *Opponents of a bill that would cut the tax on capital gains held a news conference yesterday.*

THE WAY IT SHOULD BE: *Opponents of a bill that would cut the capital-gains tax held a news conference yesterday.*

ADJECTIVES CREATED WHILE YOU WAIT Many writers, especially newspaper reporters, create ad hoc adjectives—and difficult hyphenation decisions—when a simple possessive construction would read more naturally and avoid the hyphen issue.

THE COMMON PROBLEM: *Unseasonably warm weather cut into clothing sales, hurting department store performance.*

THE LAZY PURIST'S ONE-CHARACTER CORRECTION: *Unseasonably warm weather cut into clothing sales, hurting department-store performance.*

Department store is a noun (OK, it's more complicated than that, but it *acts* as a two-word noun). While it's true that any noun can be called into service as a modifier (as *department* is in the phrase that I just simplistically called a noun), writers should avoid overusing the privilege. If the possessive works, use it.

 THE COMMON-SENSE SOLUTION: *Unseasonably warm weather cut into clothing sales, hurting department stores' performance.*

For a solution to a more extreme version of the same basic problem, read on.

AD NAUSEAM A frequently misspelled term: It's not *ad nauseum*.

ADVANCE-PURCHASE TICKETS That's *advance*, no *d*. I occasionally read about *advanced purchases*, which makes me wonder whether the buyers need to demonstrate their ability to fly the plane or sing the songs before they're permitted to complete the transaction.

AFGHANS, AFGHANIS Afghanistan's monetary unit is the *afghani*. Its people are *Afghans*, as are certain dogs and blankets.

AGENT It's usually not a formal title. FBI agents, for example, normally have the rank of special agent. Capitalize accordingly:

> *The commander of the operation was Special Agent Efrem Zimbalist Jr.*

> *The commander of the operation was agent Efrem Zimbalist Jr.*

AGES Use a numeral when stating the age of a human being or other animal in years, to acknowledge the special status our language has given numbers that follow a "to be" verb: *He's 5* is instantly understood—the *5* doesn't mean months or IQ points or feet of height. Associated Press style implies that all age-related numbers must be numerals, but it doesn't seem right to extend this privilege to inanimate objects or to months as opposed to years. Beyond 9, of course, this is a non-issue—10 and above are always numerals in AP style.

Speaking of months vs. years, beware of abandoning your journalistic objectivity in favor of sentimental ga-ga-ness when reporting the age of a very young child. Yes, the usual system of years and birthdays is inadequate to track an infant's development, but at some point it's OK to start rounding those numbers off to years. *Three months* and *six months* and *nine months* are fine, but the media's consistent references to murderer Susan Smith's children as being *3 years old* and *14 months old* struck me as absurd. *Fourteen months* old? I call that "*1*."

AIR BAGS Not *airbags*. This might change in time, but for now the term stands as two words in well-edited publications. As with all two-word compounds that many people think are one word, the hyphen is mandatory in adjectival constructions: *The air-bag controversy continues.*

ALLOTTED Not *alloted*.

ALL RIGHT Not *alright*. I'm tempted to give in on this one, as the *al-* spelling has dominated pop culture at least as long as I've been alive. From the 1960s Who classic "The Kids Are Alright" to the 1990s situation comedy "Alright Already," *all right* has been all but invisible. And it's not altogether (!) unreasonable to split off this meaning of *all right* and let it have its own spelling. *Already/all ready* and *altogether/all together* took that road, and the latter pair in particular form a precise analogy to *alright* and *all right*.

But I'm not giving in, perhaps because this is one of the classics. We word nerds have known since second grade that *alright* is not all right. You won't hear a peep from me in 2004, when all dictionaries recognize *alright* as the standard, but, as with *online*, I will not be a party to forcing the issue.

A LOT It's two words, not *alot* (a common mistake in junior-high-school newspapers).

It takes a plural verb:

A lot of people think Mary Ann was cuter than Ginger.

A lot of people will object to the vague nature of the term, but it's here to stay. When it comes to numbers, sometimes vagueness is part of the equation.

AMERICA ONLINE Be careful to avoid equating proprietary AOL content with the Internet. AOL users have access to the World Wide Web, but they are *not* on the Internet in any sense when they're in AOL chat rooms or exchanging e-mail with other AOL users. When the characters in the movie "You've Got Mail" say they met on the Internet, they're mistaken.

Proofreading note: *American Online* is starting to rival *Saudia Arabia* as the publishing world's sneakiest typo.

AMOUNTS: SINGULAR VS. PLURAL VERBS Think of the difference between discrete items and a collective quantity or amount:

> *One hundred one Dalmatians* (discrete items) *were aboard the ship.*

> *One hundred one dollars* (amount) *was paid to the captain.*

The distinction isn't always so easy. Hang on for a hair-splitting ride:

> *Ten million barrels of oil were sold.*

> *Ten million gallons of oil was sold.*

AMPERSANDS AND "AND" Most publications follow a company's preference when deciding whether to use *and* or an ampersand in a corporate name. The Wall Street Journal, oddly, changes *and* to an ampersand in an effort to standardize. I think it would make more sense to do the opposite: Change all ampersands to *and*, except when the ampersand connects initials. So it would be *Ernest and Julio Gallo* but *E&J Brandy*. One affectation that particularly bothers me is Gulf and Western's use of a plus sign in place of an ampersand. I'm tempted to call the company *Gulf Plus Western*.

AND/OR Before resorting to this clumsy device, consider whether *or* alone might mean the same thing. If you're told *Anyone who has seen or heard from this dangerous fugitive should call the FBI*, but you've both seen *and* heard from that person, does that mean you *shouldn't* call the FBI?

AND THEN I SAID . . . *And* and *but* are just as eligible as any other word for the honor of starting a sentence. And they often work well to express continuity or transition. "But I was taught never to do this," you might say. Well, you were taught wrong.

ANTI- As with *non-*, I part with many usage guides by recommending a hyphen in most cases. Both prefixes are all-purpose tools that can be tacked on to practically any word, and the non-hyphenated version of the result often isn't pretty (I see *antiabortion* and I read "anchabortion"). There's also the matter of parallelism with the antonym *pro-*, which always takes a hyphen (those who would write *antibias* don't also use *probias*). Some *anti-* combinations, however, have evolved beyond the ad hoc into words of their own, and I agree that they deserve to be written as solid: *antibody*, *antiperspirant* and *antitrust* are among those words. (The AP stylebook is right on the money on this issue; for a complete list of exceptions, buy a copy.) The ever-popular *Antichrist* is also on the list, if you're talking about the biblical villain. The adjective for "against Christ," however, is *anti-Christ*. The *Antichrist* example is instructive: The words that work well without the hyphen tend to be nouns. Even *antitrust*, which started out as an adjective meaning "against trusts," is close to noun status. It's still technically an adjective, but it's not an "against-" word (an antitrust lawyer is not a lawyer who is against trusts, but a lawyer in the field of antitrust law—a field often referred to as simply *antitrust*, which is a noun in real life if not in the dictionaries).

ANTICIPATE It means more than just *expect*. If you *antici-pate* an event, you take actions in preparation for it.

ANTICLIMACTIC *Anticlimax* and its variants pass the no-hyphen test. Also note the middle *c*; *anticlimatic* (actually, *anti-climatic*) would mean "against the weather."

ANYMORE The word should be reserved for negative statements. It should not be used as a synonym for *nowadays*.

>   **WRONG:** *A lot of people are driving sport-utility vehicles anymore.*
>
>   **RIGHT:** *You don't see people driving El Caminos anymore.*

Oh, and this should go without saying, but *any more* (two words) should be used when the meaning is "any additional."

ANYTIME Until very recently, the dictionary of choice for most newspapers called for *any time* as two words (unlike *anybody, anyhow* and *anywhere*). The fourth edition of Webster's New World College Dictionary, published in 1999, finally recognizes *anytime*.

APIECE I may be alone on this one, but I have a problem with the use of *apiece* as an all-purpose synonym for *each*. All *each*es are not created equal.

>   **RIGHT:** *The nails cost 5 cents apiece.*

Each nail constitutes one piece, and each piece costs a nickel. Fine and dandy.

>   **QUESTIONABLE:** *In 1972, AMC Gremlins started at $1,995 apiece.*

Yes, words evolve beyond their literal meanings, but Gremlins consisted of more than one piece, and I see no reason to push the issue when the perfectly good word *each* is available.

 VERY QUESTIONABLE: *Going into the 15th round, Ali and Norton had won seven rounds apiece.*

I would definitely avoid the suggestion that people are "pieces."

AREA PEOPLE What in the world are "area men" and "area women"? Reporters and editors in all media seem to have collectively decided that the word *local* should be replaced by the word *area* in all instances; I can't agree.

Where there's room, I favor *Washington-area residents* or *Boston-area residents* or whatever (note the hyphen). In headlines and other tight spots, I'd use *local residents*.

ARRESTED FOR The common construction is inherently libelous. *John Smith was arrested for bank robbery* means Smith robbed a bank and was arrested for it. Say he was *arrested on a charge of bank robbery* or *arrested in connection with a bank robbery* or something similar. Note that some jurisdictions may be picky about the word *charge*; if you're writing in a place where the charge doesn't occur until the indictment, you might want to use the *in connection with* wording or something along the lines of *arrested on suspicion of.*

ASSURE, ENSURE, INSURE The words are close in meaning, but they're not interchangeable. *Ensure* is usually the correct word; it means to "make sure": *Before starting the car, he ensures* *that the baby is buckled in. Assure* doesn't work that way; you assure *another person* of something: *After ensuring that the baby was buckled in, he assured her mother that things were fine.* One meaning of *insure* is to ensure, but better publications use the word only in references to the business of insurance: *Even if the baby isn't buckled in, her life is insured for $100,000.*

ATM It stands for *automated teller machine*, not *automatic teller machine.* And watch out for the redundant *ATM machine.*

ATTORNEYS, LAWYERS A person with a law degree is a *lawyer.* A person who acts on behalf of another person is that person's *attorney.* (Similarly, a person who acts on his own behalf in certain circumstances is acting as his own attorney.) Therefore, a lawyer can be *John Smith's attorney* or *the attorney for John Smith* or even *an attorney in the Smith case,* but nobody is *a New York attorney* or *a patent attorney* or simply *an attorney.* When in doubt, use *lawyer.*

Some people who agree with me on this distinction think lawyers use the word *attorney* the way janitors use *custodial engineer,* as a euphemism of sorts, but that isn't my point. I don't think anyone who hates lawyers feels any better about attorneys. I simply favor observing the distinction between the two words.

Helpful hint: *Attorney* is to *lawyer* as *rescuer* is to *lifeguard* (hope you got that one right on the SAT). Lawyers and lifeguards fill those roles as an occupation, but lawyers don't necessarily have clients and lifeguards don't necessarily perform any rescues. Once a lawyer signs on to represent someone, that lawyer becomes someone's attorney; once a lifeguard rescues someone, that lifeguard becomes someone's rescuer.

AUTOMOBILES It's journalistically sloppy to name a car by model alone in a hard-news story. You usually need the "make" name as well.

 WRONG: *Simpson fled in his white Bronco.*

RIGHT: *Simpson fled in his white Ford Bronco.*

In feature stories, on the other hand, informal references to well-known models work just fine:

The bar attracts the Miata crowd.

He hopped into his lovingly restored '65 Mustang and drove into the sunset.

Some journalists argue that any mention of a car's brand name constitutes unnecessary free advertising, but I disagree. When I read about a crash, I'm always curious about just what kind of vehicles were involved, and as a car buff of sorts I'm not satisfied with *convertible* or *sport-utility vehicle.*

One detail that *is* silly, however, is color. It's one thing if you're describing a car that police are hunting for (or one involved in a nationally televised low-speed freeway chase), but to routinely report that the car involved in the crash was a *blue* Ford Taurus is irrelevant.

AWACS *AWACS* is not the plural of *AWAC*; the *S* is up. It's acceptable on all references for Airborne Warning and Control System, but the acronym should be followed by *plane* or *radar plane.*

BACK TO THE FUTURE The phrase worked, more or less, in the movie, which involved time travel. Writers, apparently

"THE 5" HABITS OF HIGHLY HOLLYWOOD PEOPLE

*Interstate Highways Carry an
Intrastate Regionalism*

Movies and television series pay big money to "creative consultants"—copy editors of sorts—who are supposed to watch out for factual errors and anachronisms. I'm not one of these people, and I'm pissed. Here's why: Watch enough movies or TV and you're bound to hear a character purported to be on the East Coast say something like "They escaped on the 95." *The 95*? This is Southern California-speak.

I've heard that the *the* is used elsewhere as well, but I've lived in Michigan and Arizona and Virginia and the District of Columbia and I've never heard someone who's not in California or from California use the definite article in front of highway-designation numbers. Everywhere

continued

I've lived, it's *Interstate 95* or *I-95* or simply *95,* but never *the 95.* In California, they have *the 5* and *the 10* and *the 15.* They're not wrong; they're just different. My complaint is with those screenwriters who can't see beyond their Hollywood habitat. I could use some of that creative-consulting cash.

FREEWAY NAMES, PART 2
It's a Two-Way Street

If you take the exit marked "Interstate 66 West," are you on Interstate 66 West? No. You're driving westbound on Interstate 66. The directions on the signs are just that: directions. Freeways have lanes going in two directions, but that doesn't make them two separate freeways.

mesmerized by Michael J. Fox's performance, have been using it ever since to mean "history repeating itself," and it rarely, if ever, works. Usually what they're really talking about is "back to the past," but that isn't nearly as cute a cliche, is it? Send writers who use this phrase back to the drawing board, and don't let 'em offer DEJA VU as an alternative.

BAIL *The McKenzies were supposed to join us, but they bailed.*
Just as *cave in* is increasingly being shortened to CAVE, the phrase *bail out* is on the endangered list. Use *bail out* unless you're making a conscious effort to mimic trendy speech.

BANDANNA Dictionaries also list the *bandana* spelling, but that spelling suggests a long-*a* pronunciation—"ban-DAY-na" rather than the correct "ban-DAN-na."

BEATING THE HEAT Besides being a cliche, *beating the heat* is a silly concept when applied, as it usually is, to quaffing a sugary beverage or baking in the sun at a sweltering beach.

BEMUSED It means "confused, bewildered." It does not mean "amused."

BEST KNOWN, BEST-KNOWN This is a simple hyphenation-of-compound-modifiers issue, but it deserves mention because (a) people often get it wrong and (b) the hyphen makes a *big* difference.
For example, *the best-known sprinter* is the sprinter with the highest name recognition. This is normally the intended meaning when *best* and *known* are strung together. *The best known sprinter* is the best sprinter as far as we know. It's what you'd call the world-record holder if you wanted to make the point that, conceivably, someone somewhere who never ran competitively could be even faster.

BETWEEN, AMONG The search-and-replace types unfailingly use *between* when only two elements are involved and *among* for three or more. Steadfast adherence to this practice has been justly criticized by those who don't like the feeling of something slipping *among* their fingers, to cite one popular exception to the rule. Many critics explain the correctness of *between the fingers* by saying such slippage involves only two fingers at a time, but I think the explanation is more fundamental: *Between* is almost always the correct choice for actual physical relationships.

Sand gets *between* your toes, even if you have more than two of them. You drive *between* the pylons in driver education, no matter how many pylons there are. (You could also drive among the pylons, but that phrase leaves open the possibility of driving over them or straight down the middle in a bunch of them instead of systematically weaving between two at a time.) The two-at-a-time rule is another valid exception, however (*The round-robin tournament featured matches between the top four players*), and other exceptions include cases where multiple units are separated into two groups (*a disagreement between Bob and Carol and Ted and Alice*) and idiomatic expressions (*Let's keep this secret between the three of us*).

"BETWEEN" IS TO "AND" AS "FROM" IS TO "TO" *Monthly wages between $118 to $176* is a mixed-up construction. It's either *between $118 and $176* or *from $118 to $176*.

By the way, it is nonsense to routinely change phrases like *between 1991 and 1993* to *from 1991 to 1993*. Lots of hack editors will tell you that *between 1991 and 1993* means "in 1992." They're wrong. These editors also tend to have no problem at all with the semi-literate prose that results from such a change—phrases like *shares priced at from $20 to $24. At from?* I don't think it's possible to use those words back-to-back in a literate sentence. If *between . . . and* doesn't seem to be the right choice, use *to* with either *at* or *from*—not both. *Shares priced at $20 to $24* and *shares priced from $20 to $24* are both fine.

BLASE While "blah-ZAY" sounds much, much cooler, the correct word for "unconcerned" is *unconcerned*.

Blase (or *blasé*, if you're into accent marks) more properly refers to a state of overindulgence or world-weariness:

> *Most people would consider the French Riviera a breathtaking destination, but Guillaume had been there dozens of times and was blase about the trip.*

BOLOGNA, BALONEY *Baloney* is foolish or exaggerated talk. *Bologna* is the lunch meat, even when people (quite properly) pronounce it "baloney."

BOOKS ON TAPE Believe it or not, this is a trademark. The generic term is *audio book*. Yes, these things are *books* that are *on tape*, but the lawyers will come after us if we call them that. (What's next—Brown Pants™?)

BORDERS Use country names in their plain form when using two of them in a hyphenated construction describing a border: *the Spain-Portugal border*. Use the "of or pertaining to" descriptive form when one country is understood and only the neighboring country is being specified: *the Portuguese border*. Exception: *U.S.* (which is restricted to adjectival use by the major stylebooks) is acceptable in all such constructions, so the Canadian border could also be called *the U.S.-Canada border*.

INFINITIVES

Split Away!

A lot of editors waste a lot of time and energy making editing changes that, if you'll excuse the disgusting imagery, do nothing but shove a rod up the backside of good, conversational writing.

Perhaps the best example of this is the un-splitting fetish. No matter how many knuckles have been whacked with rulers over the "split infinitive," grammar experts will testify that there is no rule—and never has been a rule—against splitting infinitives. Somebody somewhere made up this "rule" because infinitives were never split in Latin. Of course they weren't: In Latin, infinitives are single words.

Many editors take this nonsense one step further by standing guard against anything coming between an auxiliary verb and the verb it "helps." They aren't even infinitives, and we're worried sick about splitting 'em!

Would you really call "to boldly go where no man has gone before" *wrong*? Do you really think *boldly to go* or *to go boldly* sounds better? Just as we don't change *he has not returned* to *he not has returned*, there is no need to change something like *she has never gone there* to *she never has gone there*.

Actually, I've seen this nonsense taken one more step further: Editors will unsplit things that aren't even compound verbs but at first glance look as if they are. So *it is still true* becomes *it still is true*. *True*, of course, isn't even a verb. Or the foolishly unsplit infinitive in *Hillary Rodham Clinton plans to announce formally her candidacy* gets carried over to the absurd *Clinton announced formally her candidacy*.

To review: Infinitives and other verb phrases should be written the way they sound best. Most writers are good judges of this; when in doubt, leave it alone.

BOTH AGREE Like "sharing the same," this is a minor redundancy. Agreement implies more than one person, so if you have two people agreeing, you should say *they agree*, not *both agree*. With three or four or 67 people, it's still *they* who are agreeing, not *all three* or *all four* or *all 67*.

BRITISHISMS: SAY TA-TA! A note to American editors who work with British copy: When in the Colonies, show your true colours as a subeditor, go over every dispatch as though you were kicking the tyres of a superannuated lorry with your grey plimsolls, and translate Reuters, Agence France-Presse and Deutsche Presse Agentur stories from British into *American* English. Here are just a few examples of Britishisms that frequently slip by lazy American editors.

Called: Note the Britishism in the following Reuters passage:

> *The Iranian newspaper Kayhan said a Texan called Mary Jones, 35, was arrested in a Tehran square and brought to a police station with her dog two weeks ago.*

In the U.S. of A., the woman is *named* Mary Jones. She may be *called* Jonesy or Mare-Mare or M.J. or "that woman," but in American English she is *named* Mary Jones.

Council flats: Public housing.

Frontier: Change the British word *frontier* to its American equivalent, *border*. On this side of the Atlantic, *frontier* refers to Davy Crockett stuff.

Lt.-Gen., Maj.-Gen., Lt.-Col.: Brits hyphenate such ranks; Americans don't.

Pensioner: It means "retiree."

Pyjamas: If you don't know it's *pajamas*, you should go to bed without dinner.

Sabre-rattling: Make it *saber rattling* (*e* before *r*; no hyphen unless it's a modifier).

Scheme: The word carries a connotation of nefarious or hope-lessly confused behavior in American English, whereas the British use it willy-nilly to mean *plan* or *program*.

Shop: The standard American word for "store" is *store*. The British word, also sometimes used in American, is *shop*. Since Reuters, Agence France-Presse and Deutsche Presse Agentur all write in British, we see way too many shops in copy. It's fine to say *butcher shop* and other common usages, but the word by itself denotes cutesy little curio emporiums and the like, as in *Old Town Alexandria caters to tourists with its many restaurants and shops.*

Stopping him doing, preventing him doing: In American English, we use the word *from* before *doing*.

Transport: The noun is a nice space saver, but it is a British usage and not an American one. Stick with *transportation*.

BUCK NAKED *Butt naked* is an amusing variation that has become popular, but the original expression was *buck naked*. The unadorned *naked* would seem to be naked enough for most cases, but if you must buck this advice, use a hyphen when it's a compound modifier: *A buck-naked man just ran down the street!*

CABINET SECRETARIES AND DEPARTMENTS Cabinet departments can be abbreviated on second reference by removing the *Department* or *Department of*:

> *The State Department had no comment. Sources at State said many officials were embarrassed.*

This construction causes some confusion when Cabinet secretaries' titles are used descriptively or in apposition: It's *Secretary of State Madeleine Albright* but *Madeleine Albright, the secretary of state.* Why is *state* lowercased in the second example? Because the title means "secretary in charge of affairs of state," not "secretary of the State Department." The explanation is easier to understand with a more concrete area, such as education: Think of the department and the job as being born simultaneously. The president decided there should be a Cabinet department and Cabinet secretary to deal with the issue of common-noun, small-*e* education. So the uppercased Education Department was born, and along with it the low-ercased-except-as-a-title-before-a-name education secretary.

There is one exception: Because the Treasury Department and its boss's title were named after the already-uppercased U.S. Treasury, *Treasury secretary* always gets a capital *T.*

Note that you can use *Department of Blank* interchangeably with *Blank Department*, and *secretary of blank* interchangeably with *blank secretary*, but trust your ear to avoid unfortunate-sounding constructions such as *state secretary* and *Health and Human Services Department—secretary of state* is always preferred, and the multiple-word departments generally work better with *of.*

Also, keep in mind that Cabinet secretaries aren't secretaries, just as governmental ministers aren't ministers. Take care to avoid tossing these words around in second references without their official context, as if these officials are members of the typing pool or the clergy.

CACHE, CACHET *Cache* (prounounced "cash") means "a hiding place" or "what is hidden there"; it's also a form of computer memory. *Cachet* ("cash-AY") describes a badge of quality or prestige.

CAGE, NICOLAS The actor is *Nicolas Cage*—no *h* in his first name.

CAPITALIZATION OF DEPARTMENTS, DIVISIONS AND OFFICES Sometimes offices, departments and divisions are capitalized, and sometimes they aren't. But don't do it halfway. To write *U.S. Attorney's office*, for example, or *Maricopa County Sheriff's office* implies that the words *attorney* and *sheriff* are proper nouns. They're not—as with other titles, *Sheriff Joe Arpaio* is up, but *Joe Arpaio, the sheriff*, is down.

CAPITALIZING PREPOSITIONS IN PROPER NAMES Generally, articles and prepositions of three or fewer letters are lowercase (and those of four or more letters are capitalized) in names of companies, organizations, etc., and titles of books, movies and the like:

"Gone With the Wind."

Aid to Families With Dependent Children (the fact that *AFDC* is the abbreviation makes no difference).

Books on Tape.

There are exceptions. An article or preposition should be capitalized no matter how long it is if it's:

- The first or last word in the name or title.
- Part of a unit, such as a prepositional or verb phrase, as in "The Air Up There" or the early-'80s hit song by

Dexy's Midnight Runners, "Come On Eileen" (lower-casing the *O* in that one would introduce some prurient interest, a problem exacerbated by the lack of a comma).

People's names do not follow these rules; follow the person's preference (*Arnaud de Borchgrave, Dick Van Dyke*).

CAREEN, CAREER *Careen* is a word used incorrectly far more often than it is used correctly, and this evolution is so far along that few will object to the popular usage. The word technically means "to tilt to one side," as a ship might. "To lurch or swerve speedily" is to *career*.

But, of course, when you see *careen* in print, the meaning is nearly always the latter.

Careful writers and editors face a difficult choice: Use *careen* and hear "Tsk-tsk!" from a few language snobs or use *career* and hear "Huh?" from everyone else. I'm torn, but the overwhelming prevalence of the new meaning is persuasive.

CARTER, ROSALYNN The former first lady is *Rosalynn*, not *Roslyn* or *Rosslyn* or *Rosalyn* (or *Fred*, for that matter).

CAVE The correct phrase is *cave in*, not the increasingly popular *cave*.

CELLULAR TELEPHONES I'll admit that the two formal terms side by side sound almost as quaint as *hamburger sandwich*, so I won't object to *cellular phone* or even *cell phone* on second reference—or even first reference in publications that are otherwise informal. But please keep the space, tossing *cellphone* in the same trash heap as *videogame* and *email*. Digerati need not be illiterati.

CENSUS *U.S. Census Bureau* is capitalized, but *the 2000 census* shouldn't be.

CHAIN ESTABLISHMENTS References along the lines of *at McDonald's Restaurant* lend an unfortunate Hooterville Gazette quality to writing. Acknowledge the reality of modern franchising and stick an article in front of the name of an establishment that's part of a chain:

> *She works at the McDonald's at 123 Main St.* (definite article when the location is important).

> *From her humble start as a maid at a Holiday Inn, she rose to the top of a Fortune 500 company.* (indefinite article when the location isn't important).

CHAISE LONGUE It's *longue*, not *lounge*. The term is borrowed directly from the French (literally "long chair"). I won't even get into the pronunciation issue.

CHAUVINISM, DISCRIMINATION AND DIVERSITY These words are often used as shorthand for much more specific concepts. If you mean *male chauvinism, race and sex discrimination*, and *racial, ethnic and sexual diversity*, you need to say so.

Chauvinism can refer to fanatical and blind devotion to any group or institution. When the word stands alone, that institution is generally assumed to be one's country.

Discrimination can be a very good thing—even the world's most discriminating people practice it. You don't tolerate discrimination? Then I guess you'll be fighting for the rights of the world's child-molesting day-care workers and nose-picking sandwich makers. The word should be used alone only after you've established that discrimination based on race or sex, or whatever, is what you're talking about. *Illegal discrimination* is a good catchall term, provided you're not talking about a crusade for new laws.

Diversity, similarly, can refer to any sort of mixed bag. Do you favor workplace diversity? Well, if you work with nice people, throwing in some mean ones would add diversity. If you mean diversity of race, sex and perhaps sexual orientation, say so.

CHILDREN'S Never *childrens'*. *Children* is already plural; there can be more than one child, but there can't be more than one children (although it can seem that way if you're around enough of 'em).

A CHOICE BETWEEN X AND Y Note the *and*. Especially with long sentences, there's a tendency to incorrectly write "a choice between blah-blah-blah-X *or* blah-blah-blah-Y."

Or is fine, by the way, in similar cases that don't involve the word *between*:

> *They faced a difficult choice: Starve in the Andes or eat one another.*

CLIFFS NOTES That's right, *Cliffs Notes*. I would have thought it was *Cliff's Notes*, and everyone else in the world somehow got the idea that it was *Cliff Notes*, as though writing a paper without them was like falling off a cliff.

C/O This "Man in the Gray Flannel Suit"-era mailing-address abbreviation for *in care of* should be locked in a time capsule with an adding machine, an elevator operator and

Detroit 6, Michigan. If you're writing to Bill Walsh at the Washington Post, address your correspondence to *Bill Walsh, Washington Post*. People aren't doing a whole lot of "caring" nowadays, and people who use *c/o* often don't even know what it means. I've seen letters addressed to the Washington Post "c/o" one of its staffers.

COED Don't use the word as a noun, at least not with a straight face. It's a dated, sexist term left over from the days when it was a novelty for colleges to admit women. The adjective *coeducational* is fine if it's necessary to point out that a school is not single-sex, but to label female students *coeds* while male students are simply *students* is offensive.

The adjective *coed*, meaning both sexes are involved (as in the ubiquitous "Coed Naked [NAME OF SPORT HERE]" T-shirts), is acceptable (even if the T-shirts aren't).

COLDS, COLD I'm not a doctor, but I play one on television, and it's my understanding that medical science has found no link between exposure to cold weather and the common cold. Plenty of intelligent people continue to make the connection in casual conversation, but watch out for writing that treats this common misconception as fact.

COMPANY NAMES, IN SHORT Consider the following: *Profits were up at Dell Computer and Ford Motor.*

Why not *Ford* and *Dell*? If you choose to leave off the *Co.*, *Corp.*, *Inc.*, *Ltd.* and so forth, whether as a second-reference abbreviation or as a matter of style, I think you should also leave off the attached generic words. *Ford Motor Co.* refers to a motor company named Ford, not a company named Ford Motor. *Dell Computer Corp.* is a computer corporation named Dell, not a corporation named Dell Computer. On the other hand, *General Motors Corp.* is a corporation named General Motors, as evidenced by the abbreviation *GM*, which is probably what should be used in casual references anyway.

COMPARE TO, COMPARE WITH It's true that *compare to* should be changed to *compare with* in many cases, but the truth doesn't stop there.

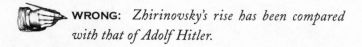 **WRONG:** *Zhirinovsky's rise has been compared with that of Adolf Hitler.*

Well, maybe it has and maybe it hasn't, but what the writer obviously meant was that his rise has been compared *to* that of Hitler.

Professors and stylebooks often explain that *compare to* is used for similarities and *compare with* is used for differences. That usually works, but it's a misleading guideline that fails to get to the heart of the distinction.

To compare something *with* something else is to point out their similarities, differences or both. To compare something *to* something else is simply to assert that they're alike, which is the meaning in this case. Think of it this way: *Compare to* means "liken to."

COMPRISED OF This is such a chestnut in the picky-about-the-language biz that you'd think people would get it right by now, but they don't. Nothing is ever "comprised of" something. *To comprise* means "to contain or to embrace":

The jury comprises seven women and five men.

All of the following mean the same thing:

The jury is composed of seven women and five men.
The jury is made up of seven women and five men.
Seven women and five men constitute the jury.
Seven women and five men make up the jury.

Even when used correctly, in my humble opinion, *comprise* and *constitute* tend to sound stilted. Some form of *is made up of* sounds better in most cases.

CONDITIONAL STATEMENTS, AS IN "WILL" VS. "WOULD"

For a thorough discussion of the subjunctive mode, get a good grammar book. Here I'll merely mention one of the most common conditional-statement errors in news writing. It goes something like this:

If he is elected, he would be the youngest mayor in the city's history.

No. If he *is* elected, he *will* be.

The confusion is understandable, as reporters are forever cautioned against stating mere proposals as matters of fact. *The project would be the city's largest*, not *The project will be the city's largest*. When an individual sentence is a conditional statement, however, both sides of the sentence need to match; in other words, the result of the condition must be taken seriously.

Another way of making both sides of the sentence match is to cast both sides in *would* mode (that is, subjunctive) instead of casting both in *will* mode. This works better with statements that can truly be called hypothetical:

If he were assassinated, he would be the city's first mayor to die in office.

CONVINCE, PERSUADE You can't go wrong observing the following rule: *Persuade* involves action, while *convince* involves thought. Thus *convince* usually goes with *of* or *that*: *She convinced him that he was wrong. He convinced her of his correctness. Persuade* usually goes with *to*: *She persuaded him to shut up.*

You'll seldom find a writer using *persuade* when it should be *convince*, and that's probably why changing *convince* to *persuade* has become part of the search-and-replace editor's repertoire. The unfortunate thing about that is that *I persuaded him I was right* sounds a lot more stupid than *I convinced him to stop*—in other words, this is a good place to bring up the Typocratic Oath: First, introduce no errors.

If you don't completely understand everything I've said on this topic, don't read on. For those of you who are ready for the advanced lesson, note that *convince* is hardly objectionable for the gentlest cases of persuasion. Teddy Roosevelt persuaded his Rough Riders to take San Juan Hill, but maybe that "Oprah" episode *convinced* Aunt Jenny to schedule a mammogram for next fall. And to confuse matters further, note that the term *persuasive speaking* can quite properly refer to oration whose goal is changing minds rather than inspiring action.

CORNET, CORONET A *cornet* is a musical instrument that is like a small trumpet. *Coronet* is a brand of paper towels endorsed by Rosemary Clooney ("Extra value is what you get/When you buy Cor-o-net!"). A coronet can also be a kind of crown or, with a capped *C*, an old Dodge.

COUNCILS AND MEMBERS City and town councils and their members cause a lot of confusion in the style department. Any editor who has worked with local news has endured plenty of made-up words (*councilmembers*) and erroneous capitalization (*the Council*).

Springfield City Council, obviously, gets three capital letters. Take away the city's name and *City Council* remains up. The word *council* alone, however, is lowercase.

If a city council (generic references are lowercase) uses the terms *councilman* and *councilwoman*, that's fine. Such terms should be up only when used as titles before a name. *City* should also be up in the latter case if it's added either as part of the title or as a clarifying element (*City Councilman Monte Geralds*). If *councilman* and *councilwoman* are not used, use the lowercased *council member*.

COUNTRIES AREN'T PEOPLE I often see phrases like *the countries who belong to the group* or *the companies who sell the product*. Unless you're specifically referring to people, *who* should be changed to *that*.

Worse yet are stories in which the reporter, no doubt looking for a little nautical flavor, refers to a country and *her people*. The personal-pronoun feminization of countries, and even ships, is a cute little custom, but it doesn't belong in serious writing.

A COUPLE OF GUIDELINES *Of* is required when *couple* quantifies an amount or time period: *a couple of hours*, not *a couple hours*. But when the word is quantifying *another quantifier*, the *of* is misplaced and the addition sounds silly: *a couple hundred people*, not *a couple of hundred people*. Placing the *of* where it really belongs sounds just as silly—you're referring to *a* *couple hundred of people*, not a couple of hundred people, whatever "hundred people" are—so it's better to just let the idiom be idiomatic.

COX ARQUETTE, COURTENEY As noted earlier, the actress really does spell her first name this way.

CUSTOMS The *U.S. Customs Service* is capitalized, but *customs* should be down in *He went through customs* and the like.

DALMATIAN The dogs are *Dalmatians*, not *dalmatians* or *dalmations* or *Dalmations*.

DAMAGE, DAMAGES *Damages* is a legal term for money paid as the result of a lawsuit. The cost of stuff trashed by a flood or a fire or whatever should be referred to with the collective noun *damage*.

DATES GONE BAD Especially in obituaries, you'll sometimes see sentences like this:

> *In 1979, he was hired as a janitor and became president of the company in 1987.*

The placement and punctuation of *In 1979* implies that all events in the sentence took place in 1979. Obviously, part of the sentence took place in 1987. Try it this way:

> *He was hired as a janitor in 1979 and became president of the company in 1987.*

DECIMAL POINTS The singular-vs.-plural-verb issue doesn't come into play with fractions (*Half an inch of rain fell. Three-*

quarters of an inch is expected tomorrow), but things get trickier when amounts greater than zero but less than one are expressed as decimals. It's obviously correct to say *0.6 of an inch of rain*, but that's not the only way to construct such a phrase. I think it's also obvious that *0.6 inches of rain* is vastly preferable to *0.6 inch of rain*, but plenty of distinguished editors would argue that the plural verb must be reserved for numbers greater than one. Starting with a baseline I think we all can agree on—that you say *zero inches* and not *zero inch*—I propose that we let go of the notion that *plural* means "more than one" and acknowledge that *singular* is singularly reserved for the unique concept of "one." Everything else, more or less, is an *amount* and gets the verb that we call, for lack of a better description, *plural*.

DEJA VU It means the feeling that you've been in a situation *when you actually have not*. It's an eerie, puzzling sensation, not a matter-of-fact observation. Robin Williams has a funny bit (well, it was funny the *first* time) in which he uses it in an ironic way when he knows full well the situation really *has* happened before. This, I theorize, was the genesis of the now-ubiquitous cliche of writers using it with a straight face to mean "history repeating itself." Don't let 'em. And don't get me started on the wholesale use of the Yogi Berra-ism (or is it Casey Stengel-ism?) "deja vu all over again." Again, cute when he said it, trite when you say it.

DEMOCRAT, DEMOCRATIC In references to the Democratic Party and its members, the noun is *Democrat* and the adjective is *Democratic*. Republicans, apparently chagrined by the favorable connotation of little-*d democratic*, have taken to saying things like "These Democrat programs are a big waste!" Sorry, but you shouldn't play politics with the language. Democratic programs are *Democratic programs.*

DEPARTING IS SUCH SWEET SORROW I keep reading that the president will depart Washington for this trip or that. What's wrong with the word *leave?* And if you must use *depart*, make it *depart from.*

DESERTS: SORRY, NO CAKE When you say someone *got his just deserts, desert* is spelled like the arid region, not the sweet treat. (Think of it this way: It's what a person *deserves*, not *desserves.*)

DIED? OR WERE THEY KILLED? *Twenty-six people died in a skirmish Wednesday in Chechnya* is a tad euphemistic, unless the death was from natural causes unrelated to the skirmish. Use *was* (or *were*) *killed* instead of *died* when a death is violent.

"DIFFERENT THAN" IS DIFFERENT FROM "DIFFERENT FROM" The search-and-replace school of copy editing holds that *different than* should always be replaced with *different from.* It ain't true, as editors who trust their collective ear should know.

Yes, *different from* is the correct choice for direct comparisons in American English. The British use *different to*, and lots of Americans without English teachers in their families grew up using *different than* in all cases (I did).

There is one case, however, that calls for *different than*, and that's an indirect comparison. (Those of you who have done their *like*-vs.-*as* homework will recognize this principle.) For example:

> *Peter Lynch has a different perspective than you and I.*

Note the *do* implied by the use of *I* rather than *me*. The comparison isn't between *Peter Lynch's perspective* and *you and I*; it's between *Peter Lynch's perspective* and *your perspective and mine*. Using *from* to make the comparison implies the former; using *than* implies the latter. Insert your own grammatical terms if you like.

Such examples could easily be rewritten to conform to the "*different from* is always right" dogma (*Peter Lynch has a different perspective from you and me, Peter Lynch's perspective is different from yours and mine*), but that doesn't invalidate the correctness of the *different than* formulation of the same idea.

It's harder to argue against the *than* when it's paired with *differently*, as in *Peter Lynch invests differently than I*. To write *Peter Lynch invests differently from me* is to commit the same error as writing *Peter Lynch doesn't invest like me*.

Or take the following:

Muhammad Ali is different today than he was in the 1960s.

Sure, you could make it *different today from how he was in the 1960s*, but why would you want to?

DISNEYLAND, WALT DISNEY WORLD *Disneyland*, the original, is in California. The one in Florida is *Walt Disney World* (*Disney World* informally or on second reference). Neither should be called *Disney*, as in *Tara Lipinski went to Disney*.

DOC MARTENS The clunky British shoes favored by the "alternative" set provide a few usage obstacles to trip over. The brand name is *Dr. Martens*—it's not *Martin* or even *Marten*. So, as with **ADIDAS**, that *s* doesn't make it a plural. The slang *Doc* in the usual *She was wearing her Doc Martens* usage is fine, but the *Martens* should, in a strict technical sense, be *Martenses*. Not that I would advise taking that route; you'll have plenty of other opportunities to look dorky in commenting on such a fashion. If at all possible, turn *Doc Martens* into an adjective: *She was wearing her Doc Martens clodhoppers.*

DOCTORS SUCH AS LAURA Physicians are doctors. People with doctorates are people with doctorates.

It's best to avoid the issue altogether, and unless your publication routinely uses courtesy titles (*Mr. Clinton met with Mr. Kohl*), it's a pretty easy issue to avoid. If Marcus Welby is a physician, say *physician Marcus Welby*. Otherwise you have to make tough decisions on where to draw the *Dr.* line. Dentists? Veterinarians? Chiropractors?

By the way, radio personality Laura Schlessinger's name is bandied about a lot these days, and it's clear that a lot of the people doing the bandying have only a vague idea of who she is. What she *isn't* is a psychologist or a sex therapist—or a doctor, for that matter. She has a doctorate in physiology and is a licensed "marriage, family and child counselor," but her radio call-in show is not about therapy; it's about issues of morality. She is a converted Orthodox Jew who takes the issue of religion very seriously—think of a kosher Jerry Falwell.

DOLLAR DOLLARS It's an easy mistake to read over: Beware of the use of a dollar sign and the word *dollars* with the same amount, as in *$100 dollars*.

DOT.COM I'll bet you "$100 dollars" that the preceding head reads "dot dot com." Stick with one dot—*dot com, dot-com* (my preference) or *.com*—in playful references to the Internet world.

DOWN PAYMENT It's two words, not *downpayment*.

DOWNTOWN In most cities it means the central business district. In Manhattan (more logically, if you think about it), it is a north-south reference—down(town) is south, and up(town) is north. Ignorant urbanophobes, to coin a word (I used to be one of them), sometimes erroneously use the word to mean any place within the actual boundaries of a big city as opposed to its suburbs. My neighborhood, Capitol Hill, is quite urban and quite centrally located, but it's a good distance from what is legitimately considered downtown Washington, D.C.

-DRIVE, HE SAID *Two-wheel-drive, four-wheel-drive, front-wheel-drive, rear-wheel-drive* and *all-wheel-drive* usually appear with two hyphens, because they usually work together as adjectives, as compound modifiers describing a type of vehicle:

> *Four-wheel-drive Toyota Tacomas are more expensive than the two-wheel-drive models.*

But there's a "but."

When *four-wheel drive* or a similar term acts as a noun, as in the concept of four-wheel drive, only the first hyphen should be used, because *four-wheel* is a compound adjective modifying the noun *drive*:

> *Many drivers prefer four-wheel drive to two-wheel drive.*

Occasionally the adjectival form is used as a noun. In this case both hyphens apply:

> *I bought myself a four-wheel-drive!*

EACH OTHER, ONE ANOTHER The classic rule is that *each other* applies to two and *one another* applies to three or more. I'm not calling for a revolt, but this seems backward: Correct me if I'm wrong, but doesn't *one* strongly imply "one," as in one plus the other equals two? Doesn't *each other* imply more than one "other"?

The advanced lesson: The plural connotation is built into these phrases, so the possessive forms are *each other's* and *one another's*, not *each others'* and *one anothers'*.

EFFETE The original meaning of *effete* is "depleted, exhausted or barren." Today the word is usually used to mean "effeminate," and it's often applied to members of the upper crust. It has been argued that the latter meaning is a return to the word's roots, but most careful writers and editors disdain such a usage. I think the gap is bridgeable: The kind of people usually described as effete have been drained of vigor by a life of privilege, and therefore they're weak in a way that comes across as effeminate.

800 NUMBERS I've always preferred *toll-free number* to *800 number*, and now I have a good reason for insisting on it: 800 isn't the only toll-free telephone prefix—it has been joined by 888 and 877, and more are on the way.

My earlier reason, aside from the possibility of major confusion ("The companies have *800* telephone numbers? Do they *need* that many?"), was probably way too picky, but here goes. I just think *800 number* has a childlike ring to it. I picture the kind of person who uses it exclusively instead of *toll-free number* as the kind of person who would hold up some fingers and say "This many!" when asked "How old are you?"

ELDERS: Y BEFORE C The former surgeon general's name is Joycelyn Elders. *Joycelyn*, with a *y*. Not *Jocelyn*. Helpful hint: Think of "the joy of masturbation."

E-MAIL Electronic mail is *e-mail*. The French word for enamel is *email*. See Chapter 3 for the full rant.

E-MAIL, PART 2: "WHAT'S YOUR EMAIL?" Well, assuming you mean *e-mail*, it's electronic correspondence sent to me (but, as they say in "Airplane," that's not important right now).

But even that isn't what you meant, is it? These days that question typically means "What's your e-mail address?" Computer messages at the Washington Post regularly ask questions like "Does anyone have Jeane Kirkpatrick's email?" (Uh, no, I don't, and I hope anyone who does will return it to its rightful owner.)

Going hand in hand with the lazy illiteracy that is robbing this word of its hyphen is the abbreviation of *e-mail address* to simply *email*. If you mean *e-mail address*, say *e-mail address*. For that matter, if you mean *e-mail message*, say *e-mail message*.

EMPLOYEE, EMPLOYE The word is *employee*. *Employe* is a remnant of a regrettable experiment in simplified spelling that saved a dime or two in newsprint and also gave us *cigaret*.

ENORMITY It wasn't always that way, etymologists will be quick to point out, but these days, educated writers and speakers reserve *enormity* for the meaning "great evil or wickedness." I think the distinction should be observed. This isn't a case like *hopefully*, where a purist's misreading of the allegedly loose usage would be relatively benign. *Enormousness* or *vastness* or *hugeness* should be substituted when the reference is simply to great size.

ENTITLED You may be entitled to see any play you want, but, in a shorter-is-better style ruling, the famous Thornton Wilder play is *titled* "Our Town." And note the lack of a comma between *titled* and the title.

AN EQUAL-HOUSING LENDER Mortgage companies bragging about their abstinence from illegal discrimination unwittingly imply that all of their customers must buy identical homes. They mean, of course, *equal-opportunity lending* or *equal housing opportunity* (still imprecise terms, but I can live with them). No illegal discrimination. Imagine that! You never hear these companies trumpeting "murder-free" policies— makes you wonder, doesn't it?

EQUALLY It works just fine without the word *as*:

 WRONG: *McEnroe was great, but Borg was equally as great.*

RIGHT: *McEnroe was great, but Borg was equally great.*

EVEN AS ... This phrase has become fashionable as an all-purpose linking transition, but it should be confined to cases in which the simultaneous occurrences present a contrast or an irony:

WRONG: *Even as Dole was delivering his concession speech, some of his supporters had tears in their eyes.*

RIGHT: *Even as he still lay in a hospital bed with two broken legs, Knievel was planning his next stunt.*

EVERYDAY, EVERY DAY *Everyday* is the adjective:

Bathing is an everyday thing for me.

Do not join the words in other situations.

 WRONG: *I bathe everyday.*

RIGHT: *I bathe every day.*

EX-, THEN-, FORMER A story tells us *former president George Bush sent more than 25,000 troops to Somalia in 1992.* Former presidents rarely have the power to do such things, and sure enough, Bush was still president in 1992. Make it *President Bush sent more than 25,000 troops to Somalia in 1992.* People generally know who the current president is. If you're dealing with a more obscure "former," take the following tack:

Then-president Vern Spalding cleaned up the custodial union. Vern Spalding, then president of the custodial union, was invited to the White House.

Note the hyphen with a *then-* usage as a label rather than an explanation.

EXPATRIATES, EX-PATRIOTS Some people living outside their country of citizenship may indeed be former patriots, but the term for all of them, patriots or not, is *expatriates*.

FALSE TITLES At the New York Times, copy editors would change *tennis legend Jimmy Connors* to *the tennis legend Jimmy Connors* under the doctrine of "false titles." To me, such a practice sounds stilted and pedantic (at least in newspaper writing). Go ahead and say *actress Julia Roberts* and *composer Marvin Hamlisch*. On the other end of the spectrum, Time magazine used to capitalize even the falsest of false titles. So it would be *Tennis Legend Jimmy Connors* and *Convicted Drug Dealer John Q. Crackhead*. I've seen some strange style practices, but I think this one was the strangest.

FAX *Facsimile* is still good for references to other kinds of reproductions, but it can be retired in favor of *fax* in references to the telephone-line graphic transmissions that have become a part of everyday life. Because of the word's short, catchy nature, a lot of people write it in all caps, as though it were an acronym. It's not an acronym, and it's not a proper noun; it should be all caps only in all-caps headings.

FEMALE, WOMEN In most cases, use *woman* as the noun and *female* as the adjective: *female soldiers, female priests*. Things like *women senators* should be confined to quotes (does anybody say "men senators"?). *Female* is OK as a noun when talking about animals, when it hasn't been established whether the person in question is a woman or a girl, and when talking about a group that includes both women and girls. If it were ever necessary to use the sexist cliche *women drivers*, that would be an exception.

50 PERCENT Unless it's being used in a statistical context alongside other percentages, why not say *half*?

FILET MIGNON It's probably my favorite steak (cool red center, thank you), so I feel a little sheepish (mmm . . . lamb!) in complaining about its rampant use, especially in cheesy Internet discourse, as a symbol of all things wonderful and luxurious ("Meeting her after all those years of loneliness was like switching from hot dogs to filet mignon"). I don't have a handy alternative cliche, but I feel obliged to point out that most gourmands would prefer a chewier, beefier cut, perhaps a rib eye or strip steak.

THE FINALS *Venus Williams defeated her sister Serena in the finals of the Lipton Championships.*

In the finals? Not unless Venus and somebody beat Serena and somebody else in the doubles final as well. Make it *the final*. Four matches make up the quarterfinals and two matches make up the semifinals, but the final is just one match.

THE FIRM *Of* is unnecessary in *the law firm of Rabinowitz, Rabinowitz and Rabinowitz.* Just make it *the law firm Rabinowitz, Rabinowitz and Rabinowitz.* Note the absence of a comma after *firm*; you'd use one only if this were the only law firm in the world. Note also that the law firm's name was borrowed from a classic "All in the Family" episode.

FIRST-COME, FIRST-SERVED Yeah, it should get hyphens when used as a modifier (*a first-come, first-served policy*, but *the policy was first come, first served*), but my main point is that you must say *served*, not *serve*. The people who are coming are the people who *are served*—they're not the people who *serve*, unless the expression is referring to the reservation policy for tennis courts. A copy editor (who later became the paper's managing editor) changed *served* to *serve* in a story I wrote when I was an intern, and I'm still holding the grudge.

FISCAL YEARS Spell out something like *the 1998 fiscal year* on first reference, but thereafter avoid usages such as *fiscal year 1998*. Write *fiscal 1998* (lowercase *f*; it's not a proper noun) and everyone will know you're referring to a year. Of course, the bureaucratic *FY 1998* should be avoided except in direct quotations.

FOLLOWING, PRIOR TO The simple words *before* and *after* are almost always preferable to their stilted cousins *prior to* and *following*. The latter, in particular, shows up in far too much copy.

Use *prior to* or *following* only in sentences where the preferable usage has already occurred:

> *He's been through such a scare before, prior to his first heart attack.*

Sometimes writers use *following* when they mean something a little more than *after*, as when they intend to imply a causal effect. *In light of* and *in the wake of* carry this implication; *following* does not.

Finally, *following* carries the risk of absurdity. The common obituary refrain *died following a heart attack* brings to mind some sage medical advice: Don't follow heart attacks.

FOR MY PART . . . You don't have to do much reading to come across sentences like this:

For his part, he declined to comment.

For her part, she referred reporters to a news release.

For their part, they contributed $500 in the victim's name to the National Hula Hoop Society.

For *whose* part? Certainly not the readers'. And what exactly is this *part* we're always hearing about? I have yet to see a sentence in which this device did anything but waste space.

FOUNDERING, FLOUNDERING The search-and-replace school of editing assumes every use of the verb *flounder* is a mistaken attempt to say *founder*. *Flounder* might have originated through such confusion, but its meaning is sufficiently different to justify keeping the word around. To founder is to sink; to flounder is to struggle clumsily, like a fish out of water. So if you're sure a company is going under, it's foundering; if there's an outside chance it could right itself, it's floundering.

FRACTIONS Use fraction symbols abutting a numeral for numbers that include fractions: *1¾, 2½*. Please note, however, that fraction symbols are not to stand alone. If there's no whole number to attach, you must write out *one-half, three-eighths*, etc.

Do not write out *two-and-one-half*, even in quotes. People whose speech otherwise betrays not a hint of pretension take pains to say *two and ONE half* when they mean *2½*. Use the latter configuration for numbers that include fractions, with a numeral abutted by a true fraction, even in quotations (there's no pronunciation difference). If the number must come at the beginning of a sentence, write *Two and a half.*

-FREE The suffix in *tax-free* and the like should always get a hyphen, whether the compound appears before or after the term it refers to:

> *The fat-free frozen yogurt is also sugar-free.*

FRESHMAN, FRESHMEN Don't pluralize *freshman* as an adjective. It's *freshman Republicans*, not *freshmen Republicans*, just as it's *sophomore biology majors*, not *sophomores biology majors*.

FRIG, FRIDGE *Frig* is a mild curse word: *I don't give a frig about the friggin' Redskins.*

Fridge is short for *refrigerator*: *Former defense secretary William "The Refrigerator" Perry, who also played for the Chicago Bears, prefers to be called "Fridge."*

I'm still checking on reports that there are actually two famous William Perrys.

A "FROM" NEEDS A "TO"

 RIGHT: *He defended the title six times during his 1964-1967 reign.*

WRONG: *He was the champion from 1964-1967.*

Time spans can be expressed conversationally (*from 1964 to 1967*) or as units (*1964-1967* or *1964-67*), but those forms shouldn't be mixed. Once you start with the conversational *from*, you're committed to using a *to*. If you must express a span as a unit in conversational writing, replace the *from* with an *in*:

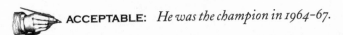 **ACCEPTABLE:** *He was the champion in 1964–67.*

See the "BETWEEN IS . . ." entry for more on the misuse of *from . . . to.*

GENDER, SEX Well-intentioned but misguided traditionalists (*paging G. Gordon Liddy . . .*) will harrumph that *gender* is purely a grammatical term and that *sex* should be used in all references to the differences between males and females. That rule might have worked back when the word *sex*, meaning "sexual intercourse," wasn't being tossed around casually by the mass media. Today, however, it's difficult to write a day's worth of news without employing *gender* in a case where *sex* might be misunderstood.

For example, with affirmative action in the news, stories often discuss "race and sex preferences." When I see *sex preferences*, I think of *sexual preferences*, as in the issue of homosexuality, not hiring practices favorable to women. Words evolve when they need to, and *gender* needed to.

An evolution of *gender* that I'm not willing to accept is its politicization. People who contend that no sexual behavior should be considered unusual have adopted the word to express such thoughts as *Johnny is a member of the male sex, but he likes to wear dresses, so he's of the female gender.*

GOD If you're writing for the church bulletin, *He* and *Him* and *His* are fine. Otherwise, lowercase the personal pronouns.

GOURMET No, I'm not here to lecture anyone on when the proper word is *gourmand.* My point is that *gourmet* is a silly, 1950s-sounding word that is usually best avoided. Referring to *a gourmet chef* or *a gourmet restaurant* is the same sort of damning-by-label that makes a "humor" heading on a news-paper or magazine article unintentionally humorous. The piece is either funny or unfunny, and either the food tastes good or it doesn't. When I was 8 or 9, I fancied myself as committing gourmet-osity when I diverted the cinnamon-sugar shaker from my applesauce to my pork chops. America's taste buds have done a lot of growing up since the days when expensive meals were necessarily pretentious, and while you won't find a lot of Jell-O molds at top-notch restaurants, you just might pay $20 or $30 for a big-time chef's interpre-tation of meat loaf and mashed potatoes. Is that *gourmet*? Does it matter?

What prompted me to rant about this word was a radio ad for lozenges that supposedly suppress the appetite. The voice-over called them "gourmet lozenges." *Lozenges!* Even if the darn things were foie-gras-flavored, how could a *lozenge* be "gourmet"? Sure enough, seconds later the ad specified that the things "taste great—like candy!" Ah. What could be more gourmet than hard candy?

GRADES Use *A-minus*, *C-plus*, etc., (not *A−*, *C+*) when men-tioning letter grades. Note, also, the absence of quotation marks. Use an apostrophe with plurals of single letters; oth-erwise *A's* will look like the word *As*. Letter grades, unlike letters used as letters, should be set in roman type. (See LET-TERS AS LETTERS.)

GRADUATION I'm in the middle on this one. It's undeniably Jethro-esque (though increasingly popular) to say *He graduated high school*. Then again, I'm not one of those old-timers who insist it should be *He was graduated from high school*. Make it *He graduated from high school*.

GRAFTING A car commercial advertises *special APR financing*. The implication that there's something called *APR financing* is an example of what I call a graft, with the modifier *APR* (annual percentage rate) plucked from its rightful position (attached to a number) and affixed to the noun it's supposed to modify. Unlike the legitimate graft that occurred when the lines on a football field became YARD LINES, it's obvious that *APR* should be attached to *1.9* in the phrase *1.9 APR financing*. Change *APR* to *percent* and it becomes even more obvious.

REALISTIC CONVERSATION: *"What kind of financing are they offering?" "It's 1.9 APR!"*

NOT SO REALISTIC: *"What kind of APR financing are they offering?" "It's 1.9!"*

GROW Avoid using *to grow* as a transitive verb meaning "to expand" or "to increase the size of." As a transitive verb it means "to raise or cultivate," as in vegetables.

WRONG: *Andre Agassi grew tennis as a spectator sport.*

WRONG: *The newspaper is trying to grow its circulation.*

RIGHT: *The newspaper's circulation grew.*

RIGHT: *Oliver Douglas grew apples.*

GUERRILLA Not *guerilla*.

HACKERS Avoid using the term *hacker* to refer to computer enthusiasts in general (picture a local-TV newscaster: "Seven-year-old Jared Smith is a real hacker. He plays Tetris three hours a day!"). One meaning of *hacker* is "extremely proficient programmer," but in popular usage it is often read to mean someone who, as a hobby or for criminal purposes, figures out how to thwart systems' security measures and break in. The geek brigade is quick to point out that *cracker* is the proper term for hackers with nefarious intent, but most publications are read by an audience largely composed of non-geeks. Use *cracker* if you like, but be sure to explain it.

HARDY, HEARTY The words are often confused, as both have among their meanings "robust" and "healthy."

Hardy means "strong, durable, capable of withstanding difficult conditions," as in *the hardy mountain climbers. Hearty* also means "strong," but it's active where *hardy* is passive; *hearty* is the word that belongs in expressions such as *hearty applause*, *a hearty meal* and *a hearty appetite*.

HEIGHT One of my earliest peeves, dating from elementary school: *Width* and *breadth* are words, but *heighth* is not a word. Use plain old *height*.

HELLO TECHNOLOGY? As a noun, it's *high technology* or *high tech*. As an adjective, it's *high-technology* or *high-tech*. It's never *hi tech* or *hi-tech*.

HERE It might not look like it, but this can be one of the most pretentious words in the language. Self-important foreign (and even domestic) correspondents are fond of saying that *analysts here* are saying this and *newspapers here* are reporting that, forcing readers to glance back at the dateline to figure out what the heck the writer is talking about. I don't care how big *JOHANNESBURG* or *NOVI SAD* or *MONTE-VIDEO* might be at the top of your story; please have the courtesy to write *analysts in Johannesburg* or *newspapers in Novi Sad* or *taxi drivers in Montevideo* if you give a hoot about your readers.

HIGH COURT At least in the United States, it's not the name of any court, though it can be used, lowercased, as a synonym for *Supreme Court.*

HIKE The common ban on using *hike* to mean "increase" doesn't make much sense to me. Sure, a hike is a long walk. But it's also an increase. You can't outlaw the concept of multiple meanings.

HIT MAN Two words, pronounced "HIT MAN," if you're referring to a hired killer. One word, pronounced "HITmun," if anybody is unfortunate enough to have it for a last name ("We've been invited to the Hitmans' for dinner!").

HIV It's the *human immunodeficiency virus*, so *HIV virus* is redundant.

HOME AND HONE You can hone a skill, but you can't hone in on something. The term is *home in.*

HOME PAGE First, it's *home page*, not the ghastly *homepage* (which begs to be pronounced "HOME-pudge" or "huh-MEP-pudge"). Use the term with caution, if at all, as it is used to mean a variety of things. Some people use it synonymously with *Web page* or *Web site*; others use it to mean a person's personal Web site or even a company's "identity" site; still others use it to mean the main page within a Web site.

It's the last meaning that makes the most sense, and a clear reference such as *the home page of the Dow Chemical Web site* helps to prevent confusion. (See also WORLD WIDE WEB.)

HOPEFULLY Use of the word to mean "it is to be hoped that" instead of "while full of hope" marks the speaker or writer as illiterate in many eyes, and that's too bad. It's not clear why *hopefully* has such a stigma attached to it when other words that work the same way (*frankly* comes to mind) don't raise an eyebrow.

My advice? *I* won't complain if you use *hopefully* the way most people do, but be prepared to hear a lot of other people gripe. Personally, I avoid this usage, if only to avoid the scorn of the misinformed legions.

HOST Well-intentioned but misguided traditionalists will tell you *host* should not be used as a verb. The trouble is, there's no equivalent verb. Holding an affair isn't always the same thing as hosting one, and *play host to* is unnecessarily wordy and stilted. *Host* fills a void and makes a fine verb.

HOUSES, HOMES With "A house is not a home" as their mantra, many copy editors change *home* to *house* in all references to residential quarters. Often this is wise: *House* is the more precise term when that's what the writer is writing about, and *home* often creeps in because that's the word the real-estate industry likes to use.

But don't add this to your automatic-search-and-replace list. Also for reasons of precision, *home* is the better term in catchall references to households or places of residence. Plenty of people without houses have homes, whether they be apartments, trailers, houseboats or none of the above.

HOWEVER, . . . Strunk and White caution against beginning sentences with the word, and I must admit I reflexively follow this advice, although close inspection reveals it to be a silly taboo.

The argument is that when you see *however* at the beginning of a sentence, you read it not as meaning "but," but as meaning "in whatever way":

However I try to change this tire, I always fail.

This logic flies out the window, however, when you realize that the latter meaning *never* takes a comma, while the former one *always* does. Confusion resolved.

ICEBOX, TINFOIL AND OTHER RELICS In these newfangled times, we have *refrigerators* and *aluminum foil*. In speech, the Ralph Kramden-ization of the language is merely annoying; in writing, it's almost criminal. (Would you trust the reasoning of someone who thinks it's 1953?)

I COULD CARE LESS Some language mavens have attempted to justify *I could care less*, but the expression is an error, plain and simple. It's not sarcasm, and it's not a shortened form of *I could care less, but I don't!* It's an unsuccessful attempt to get across the point *I couldn't care less*.

IDIOMS The whole point of using idioms is that everybody knows what they mean. So it's especially grating to see one misused. This happens with some regularity in newspaper

SLOPPY SIMILES

Why Does Paul McCartney Want Me to Live on His Piano?

In his schmaltzy but beloved hit song, Paul McCartney talks of ebony and ivory living in harmony on his piano keyboard and then wonders, "Oh, Lord, why don't we?"

Why don't we live side by side on Paul McCartney's piano keyboard? I can think of several reasons, but my point is that sloppiness in similes and other comparisons is a common fault in writing. Often such comparisons take the form of a factually correct statement that fails to make the intended point:

> *For the first time in HUD history, a Cleveland public-housing project was free of reported crime for an entire month.*

A sharp editor would ask the reporter whether this was the first time any HUD hous-

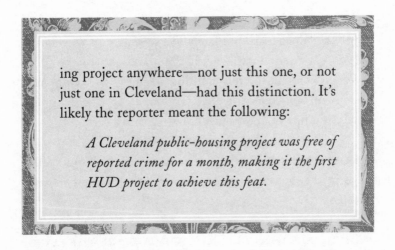

ing project anywhere—not just this one, or not just one in Cleveland—had this distinction. It's likely the reporter meant the following:

A Cleveland public-housing project was free of reported crime for a month, making it the first HUD project to achieve this feat.

leads, but the best example I can think of is from a radio commercial for a spanking-new vitamin formulation:

You weren't born yesterday. Why take a multivitamin that was?

The stupidity of this slogan might not be apparent right away, because *yesterday* can conjure different images depending on the time frame it occupies. Observe: When you say "I wasn't born yesterday," *yesterday* has a literal connotation—you're saying you are old enough to know a thing or two. But the commercial tries to have it both ways by keeping the idiom but pulling a switcheroo by using *yesterday* to mean, essentially, *yesteryear*—or at least yesterday as old rather than new, as in *yesterday's news*. In fact, this new, improved vitamin *was* "born yesterday"; it's just that such freshness means a good thing when it comes to technological advances as opposed to the depth of a human's cumulative experience.

IMPACT Careful writers know that *impact* should be avoided as a transitive verb. While teeth may be impacted, the Federal

Reserve Board's decisions on interest rates *affect* the economy; they don't "impact" it. But lately I've seen a lot of writers and editors get carried away with their aversion to the word *impact*. There's absolutely nothing wrong with saying Alan Greenspan and company *have an impact on* the economy. *Impact* is a fine noun; it's just not a transitive verb.

IMPOSTOR This is perhaps the most commonly misspelled word in the language—it's *impostor* with an *o*, not *imposter* with an *e*.

INDIVIDUALS WHO NEED INDIVIDUALS ARE THE LUCKI-EST INDIVIDUALS IN THE WORLD The word is *person*, not *individual*, unless there's an overriding need to distinguish the person you're referring to from a multiple-person unit.

INFORMATION, AS IN "MORE INFORMATION" In many publications you'll see sentences like *More information is available by calling 555-1234.*

Available by calling? I'm afraid I haven't been introduced to the person who would be doing the calling.

This construction stems from a taboo that many publications have against "addressing the reader." Misguided, I say. My preferred style: *For more information, call 555-1234.*

INITIALISMS ARE UP, BUT THE WORDS MAY BE DOWN Yes, *AIDS* and *HTML* and *ATM* are all caps. But that doesn't mean *acquired immune deficiency syndrome, hypertext markup language* and *automated teller machine* are.

INITIALS: NO SPACE I'm *W.F. Walsh*, not *W. F. Walsh*, if you choose to refer to me by my first and middle initials. This is

MONIKER LEWINSKY

Middle Initials Sometimes Get in the Way of Common Sense

When I studied journalism at the University of Arizona, one of the first things I was taught was the supreme importance of middle initials. If a student turned in a story that mentioned a non-middle-initialed person, a failing grade would be automatic. After all, the professors said, if you write about the arrest of John Smith, you're risking a libel suit from the John M. Smiths and John P. Smiths who aren't the John Q. Smith who was arrested. OK, fine, I get it. And then, before I could turn in a story that mentioned "Roots," I spent hours gathering evidence that Alex Haley had no middle name. I was still nervous—this loophole hadn't been explicitly spelled out—but apparently there was an exception when the middle initial was nonexistent.

continued

Heavy sigh. When *I'm* in charge, I vowed, there will be a limit to this nonsense.

Well, UofA apparently isn't the only school that teaches this principle, and my fellow students apparently had the opposite reaction—joining their tormentors rather than rebelling. (Ever hear of the Stockholm syndrome?)

So now I read newspapers, including my own, that write about "the Monica S. Lewinsky scandal." As opposed to the Monica G. Lewinsky scandal.

Middle initials can be fine and wonderful things. Write "William Buckley" and you'll have readers scratching their heads and asking, "Is that the same person as William *F.* Buckley?"

But not everybody is known by a middle initial. My driver's license says *William F. Walsh*, but my public identity, if I can be said to have one, is *Bill Walsh. William F. Walsh* would be accurate, but plenty of people who know my work wouldn't recognize the reference, and *Bill F. Walsh* would be just plain wrong. (To go slightly off topic, I contend that calling me *William Walsh* without the middle initial is almost as bad.)

I understand where *Monica S. Lewinsky* came from. Newspapers—especially "papers of record" such as the New York Times and my employer, the Washington Post—wisely avoid taking liberties with people's names, and this means favoring the formal over the familiar unless the person has expressed a preference for a shortened form or nickname (Jimmy Carter, Ted Turner, Bill Clinton). Occasionally a person prefers the dignity of formal address to a more familiar public identity (Ted Kennedy is Edward M. Kennedy in any decent newspaper), and that's fine. People should be called what they want to be called, within reason (I reserve the right to invoke the Freakin' Weirdo Clause when such a request is not within reason—see Chapter 3).

In the Lewinsky case, however, in which there was no public statement of middle-initial preference, I see no reason to scurry around and dig up the middle initial of a distinctively named figure in the news and use it to clutter and obscure that distinctive, widely known name. If this *S* is so darn important, what does it stand for? Does anyone know? To write *the Kenneth W. Starr investigation of the Monica S. Lewinsky scandal* is akin to writing *Las Vegas, Nev.-style gambling* or *the [Muhammad] Ali [formerly Cassius Clay] shuffle*. (And even if your

continued

paper's style is utterly rigid on the letter of the
law, why not strike a small blow for conversational writing and simply avoid the issue when
the name is adjectival? Write *the Lewinsky affair*
and save Monica and her cute little *S* for a noun
reference.)

If you're writing about unknown subjects
and there's a risk of misidentification, be as specific as possible, including middle initials. By all
means use *George W. Bush* to distinguish him
from the other George Bush. But if you're writing about Monica S. Lewinsky or Jesse L. Jackson, spare us the alphabet soup.

another newspaper style custom dictated by dated typesetting
considerations (papers don't want a line break to come
between the initials), but I think it's here to stay—even
though computerized typesetting has made it easy for most
papers to avoid such a break. The *W. [pause] F.* style looks
antiquated, in my humble opinion, though it is still in style in
many quarters of scholarly and book publishing.

INTERNET, NET It's the *Internet*, not the *internet*. I've heard
impassioned arguments against the capital *I*, but I must disagree. Sure, it's not a brand name, but it's every bit as much a
proper noun as, say, *White House* or *Dewey Decimal System*.

The shortened form should also be capitalized. I prefer *Net* (no apostrophe), but *'Net* would be a defensible stylistic choice.

INTO, ONTO The distinctions between *into* and *in to*—and between *onto* and *on to*—are quite confusing, as the definition of the one-word formulations is the two-word formulations. The important thing to keep in mind is that idioms ending in *in* and *on* should be preserved. So it's *logging on to the Internet*, not *logging onto*. And the absurdity of *The suspect turned himself into police* should be readily apparent.

INTRANET Lowercase *intranet*, which refers to a network of HTML pages within a company, organization or other computer network considerably smaller than the worldwide Internet.

Avoid the term *Web* in connection with an intranet. Intranet documents are virtually indistinguishable from Web pages, but they aren't actually on the World Wide Web. Use *intranet page* or *intranet site*. Also, to prevent confusion with the Internet, do not shorten *intranet* to *net* or *'net*.

INTRODUCTORY CLAUSES When in doubt, use a comma: *In 1971, Joe Frazier defeated Muhammad Ali.*

The comma can be omitted when things are short and breezy or, especially, when parallelism is needed and extra punctuation would muck things up (*Yesterday she had her tonsils removed; today she's eating a lot of ice cream*). It should never be omitted when it serves to separate two capitalized words (*In January, Amalgamated Industries announced a large-scale restructuring*). Don't leave your readers wondering what *January Amalgamated* is.

IRONIC The Alanis Morissette song spurred a chorus of word nerds to tell us that, basically, *nothing* actually qualifies as ironic. I agree that the song (ironically, some would say) is virtually irony-free, although "a no-smoking sign on your cigarette break" comes pretty close. Oddly (ironically, some would say), Alanis doesn't commit the usual error of substituting *ironic* for *coincidental* or *interesting*; her examples (rain on your wedding day?) are more along the lines of "bad," a concept that is more often mislabeled TRAGIC. What *is* truly ironic? The example I like to use is someone being killed in a car crash on the way to a safe-driving award ceremony.

IT'S ONE OF ITS BIGGEST PROBLEMS Do I really need to waste ink on this? If you've come this far, surely you know that *its* is the possessive form of *it*, whereas *it's* is a contraction of *it is* (or sometimes *it has*). You didn't know that? Then I'll stop calling you "Shirley."

JURY-RIGGED, JERRY-BUILT I decided to include this because people always forget which one is *-rigged* and which is *-built*, but it should also be pointed out that the meanings aren't quite identical.

Jury-rigged means "put together for emergency use." *Jerry-built* means "built cheaply and shoddily." In other words, something jury-rigged with great skill (the air purifier on Apollo 13, for example) would not qualify as jerry-built.

KANSAS CITY: WHICH ONE? Neither of the Kansas Citys should be mentioned alone, without its state, on first reference.

Why not let the much bigger Missouri city stand alone? Well, it *is* much bigger than the Kansas city, but the smaller city has the advantage of being its state's namesake. Most readers would understand that *Kansas City* means Missouri, but others might think the state was left off the Kansas city to avoid the redundancy. Avoid the issue: Use the state.

D.C.-area residents will recognize a similar problem with Fairfax County (huge) and Fairfax City (tiny). Does *Fairfax* alone mean the city (counties usually take the word *county*, and besides, *Fairfax* on a Beltway sign means the city), or are we to assume that any reference that familiar must be to the larger entity? Nobody knows. Specify in all cases.

KAZAKHSTAN It's spelled with an *h*. The former Soviet republic decided to drop the letter at one point, but it then switched back. The people of Kazakhstan are *Kazakhs*, and the adjectival form is *Kazakh*.

KIDS I wouldn't use the word to mean "children" in, say, a doctoral thesis, but the ever-popular objection to its informal use ("Do ya mean *goats*?!?") belongs in the assisted-living facility, if you know what I mean.

KILLED AFTER . . . Beware of cop-shop reportage phrased like this:

A man was killed after his car struck a tree.

Did somebody shoot him? If the crash inflicted fatal injuries, then he was killed *when* (or *died after*) his car struck a tree. *Fatally injured* would be better than *killed* if he hung on for any length of time.

KUDOS It's a Greek word used as a synonym for *praise*, and it happens to end in an *s*. But it's not a plural. There's no such thing as "a kudo." I agree with most usage experts, who'd prefer to avoid the issue by ditching the pretentious term altogether.

KU KLUX KLAN It's *Ku*, not *Klu*. Smart people know this already, as do some extremely stupid people (that is, members of the organization), but a lot of folks in between have a hard time with the "one of these words is not like the others" concept.

L DOES NOT EQUAL ONE Sorry to pick on the old-timers, but far too many haven't gotten the clue that these newfangled computers aren't 1934 Olivettis and thus the lowercase *L* key should not be used in place of the numeral *1*. It doesn't look all that bad on the screen, but in most typefaces used in newspapers, magazines and books it looks positively dreadful.

LAG It isn't properly used as a transitive verb, despite all you've read about your mutual fund *lagging the S&P 500 index*. A fund can lag *behind* the index, or it can simply *lag*, but one thing can't lag something else.

LAST, NEXT, THIS PAST, THIS COMING When it's April and I read that something happened *last March* or *last February*—or that something is going to happen *next May*—I have absolutely no idea what that means. I might as well flip a coin. Technically and literally, last March was less than a month ago and next May is less than a month in the future. But why on earth would a writer use such a distant term for something so close? So maybe *last March* means March of last year. Only the writer knows. If something happened in March of this year and the story is going to be published in April of this year, it should read *in March* or *last month* (same with *in May* or *next month*). If something happened in March of last year and the story is going to be published in April of this year, it should read *in March [insert year here]*. It's perfectly appropriate to say *last April*, though, when referring to April of last year in a story to be published in April of this year, or *next April* in a story being published the previous April.

Similarly, the familiar informal terms *this, this past* and *this coming* should be avoided in print. *This Monday, this past Monday* and *this coming Monday* all can be indicated quite clearly with the correct verb tense and *Monday. Not this Monday, but next Monday* can be indicated with the date or, if the colloquial touch is desired, *a week from Monday*.

LAST, PAST A minor point, but I prefer *in the past five years* to *in the last five years*, to avoid the implication that something (perhaps time itself) is on its last legs.

LEAGUE STANDINGS On second references that use just a part of a group's name, follow this guideline: Lowercase if the reference makes sense as a generic word; uppercase if it doesn't. Examples:

The Central Intelligence Agency is an agency, so *agency* is lowercase when used alone.

Baseball's American League is a league, so *league* is lowercase when used alone.

The Arab League and the Urban League are not what would normally be called leagues in modern American English; they're organizations. So *League* should be uppercase when used alone.

THE "THE": PUT THAT DOWN!

*Know an Article's Rightful Owner Before
You Decide Whether to Capitalize*

"Welcome to The Gazette staff," began a very
welcome letter I received late in my senior year
of college. It wasn't the time or the place to get
nitpicky, but that sentence contained one of my
many pet peeves.

The goes with *staff*, not *Gazette*. So, regardless of whether the Phoenix Gazette's style was
to cap its *The*, that particular capitalized *the* was
just plain wrong. But you see it more often than
not in references to *The Post article* or *The Times
newsroom*. The underlying principle here is that
articles (*a*, *an*, *the*) are often deleted from names
and titles when those names or titles find themselves in adjectival roles (a star of "The Brady
Bunch" is a *"Brady Bunch" star*, and a reporter

for the Press-Democrat is *a Press-Democrat reporter*).

If you're not convinced that this wayward capital *T* is an egregious error, consider that it's precisely analogous to capitalizing the word *bill* in the sentence *American Express is going to bill Walsh for his purchases.* That *bill*, like *the* in the other examples, is an unrelated word that, coincidentally, found itself next to a word it often *is* related to.

This phenomenon fits rather nicely with my theme of the dangers of search-and-replace editing. It's easy to imagine editors learning of a "We capitalize our *The*" decree and using the search-and-replace function to change every *the Gazette* to *The Gazette*.

LET ME BE, LEAVE ME ALONE The puzzling thing here is how the aberrant *Leave me be* and *Let me alone* ever got used in the first place. My guess is that it's the similarity of the two correct phrases; as with *I could care less*, people don't give a lot of thought to the content of their annoyed exclamations.

The grammar part is easy: *Let me be* is correct. Of course you can allow someone to be. But how could you allow someone to *alone*? On the other hand, you could certainly leave someone alone, just as you could leave someone here, there or anywhere. But leaving someone *be*? I don't think so.

Many people insist that *Let me alone* is not only correct but also *mandatory* in cases where the meaning is "Stop bothering me" as opposed to the literal "Leave me by myself." I guess we have a case of dueling idioms here: I say *Leave me alone* nearly always means "Stop bothering me"; it would sound funny to use the phrase literally, even though the meaning would be clear. But *Let me alone* is gibberish. It's grammatically analogous to saying *Allow me to purple!*

LETTERS AND THE LAW To *the* or not to *the*; that is the question. It may seem inconsistent for a sentence to mention *OSHA and the EPA*, but that would be the correct way to mention the two shortened forms. Here's why:

True acronyms—initials that are pronounced as words, as opposed to letter by letter—don't need the article *the*, so OSHA is *OSHA* and NATO is *NATO* and NHTSA (the National Highway Traffic Safety Administration) is even *NHTSA*, because most people pronounce it as "nitza," not as "N-H-T-S-A." The preferred pronunciation also affects the *a*-vs.-*an* decision: It's "a Nitza ruling," but it would be "an N-H-T-S-A ruling."

That "most people" criterion can become a close call. I say R-O-T-C and U-R-L when I'm referring to the Reserve Officers' Training Corps or a uniform resource locator, but lots of people say "rot-see" and "earl." So publications where I'm in charge will say *an ROTC unit* and *a URL*, but your mileage may vary.

With initialisms that aren't acronyms, the same rules apply to the full name and the shortened version. *International Business Machines Corp.* doesn't take a *the*, so neither does *IBM*. The Environmental Protection Agency, on the other hand, is *the EPA*. The federal Bureau of Alcohol,

Tobacco and Firearms has two common abbreviations, and they illustrate my point. If you use *BATF*, you need a *the* (it's "the bureau"), but if you use *ATF*, as I do, you don't (it would make no sense to call the bureau "the Alcohol, Tobacco and Firearms").

One possible exception that comes to mind is references to universities. Arizona State University, obviously, is *ASU*, but is the University of Arizona necessarily the *UofA*, or *the UA*? I don't think so—I can live with *UofA* just as easily as *the UofA*, and while I don't like either *UA* or *the UA*, I prefer the former.

LETTERS AS LETTERS Quote marks? Italics? Apostrophes with plurals? Uppercase? Lowercase? Letters used as letters present a host of typographical choices. For the purposes of this book, which discusses the issue a heck of a lot more than any newspaper would, I've used italics, not quote marks, and tailored the case (upper vs. lower) to the situation. I'm minding my *p*'s and *q*'s, using apostrophes with plurals of single letters, as many stylebooks advise, to avoid such potential pratfalls as rendering the plurals of *a* and *i* as funny-looking versions of the words *as* and *is*. See also GRADES.

LETTERS AS SHAPES Many publications, books in particular, will switch to as plain a sans-serif typeface as possible when a writer uses a letter to describe a shape. So a pipe becomes U-*shaped*, not *U-shaped*, and a ranch-style house is L-*shaped*, not *L-shaped*. This practice is downright silly; we're talking prose here, not an architectural blueprint. If I tell you my girlfriend's mouth formed the shape of an *O* when I presented her with her fabulous diamond-and-emerald engagement ring, I'm simply drawing a rough alphabet-shaped analogy—

whatever *O* we're using in the surrounding text will do just fine. If I had meant to present you with a precise artist's rendering, I would have pointed you to Figure 1(a).

LICENSE PLATES Those metal things on cars are *license plates*. Avoid calling them *tags*, which more properly refers to the stickers that revalidate them from year to year.

LIGHT-YEARS A light-year is a measure of distance, not of time. And please note the hyphen.

LIKE, AS I'll do my best to explain this one without too much English-teacher jargon. *Like* works just fine if you're making a direct comparison: *I'm just like Bjorn Borg.* Or *My forehand is like Borg's.* Or even *It's like taking candy from a baby* (*taking candy from a baby* is a phrase that acts as an object—a noun of sorts). But once the object of the comparison acquires its own verb, *as* is needed: *I hit my forehand as Borg does.*

I'm just old enough to remember TV before cigarette advertising was banned, and one classic was Winston's "What do you want, good grammar or good taste?" campaign. The jingle would go "Winston tastes good, like a cigarette should," and a voice would correct: "Winston tastes good *as* a cigarette should." (They never got around to mentioning that smoking is for dupes.)

LIKE, SUCH AS This distinction is ignored by many fine writers, but I think it is worth observing: The phrase *players like Borg, Connors and McEnroe* can be read as excluding the very players it mentions. If the meaning is "Borg, Connors, McEnroe and players like them," you could phrase it just like that, or you could write *players such as Borg, Connors and McEnroe*. (Not that there are many players "like" any of them.)

Like is fine, by the way, when an example is obviously made up, as in "phrases like *between 1991 and 1993*."

LOAN, LEND This is yet another etymologically hazy distinction, but educated writers of contemporary English prefer *loan* as the noun and *lend* as the verb. In other words, if you don't wish to incur the word nerds' wrath, give up *loaned* for *lent*. (TV-savvy readers will recall that Meathead corrected Archie Bunker on this very point. For the pathologically TV-savvy, this parenthetical aside will bring to mind the definition of *kumiss*.)

LOATH, LOATHE *Loath* is an adjective meaning "reluctant":

He was loath to accept a pay cut.

Loathe *is a verb meaning "to hate":*
He loathed his job and set out to find a new one.

A LOCAL (OR AREA) HOSPITAL If an injured person is taken to a hospital 300 miles away, that's worth noting. Otherwise, the reader is safe to assume *local* and you're safe to skip the cliche.

MAJORITY RULE If the Senate votes 66-34 in favor of a proposed constitutional amendment, one short of the required two-thirds majority, it is wrong to write *The amendment was rejected 66-34*. You can't say it was *approved* either, but that's easy to get around, as I did in the first sentence of this entry.

MAKE IT CLEAR Use the *it*. It's become fashionable of late to write things like *He tried to make clear that he was not stepping down.*

MALTS Not all milkshakes are malts. A malted milk, or *malt*, is a shake with a spoonful of that magical powder that cuts the sweetness with a tinge of, well, maltiness.

This isn't a huge point of contention in the language business, of course, but it sticks in my mind because of a Steve Martin routine in which the otherwise brilliant comedian dropped a few notches in my book by talking about malts at McDonald's. McDonald's doesn't serve malts. Neither does Burger King, Wendy's, Hardee's, Jack in the Box or Arby's. They all serve shakes, except for Wendy's, which offers an edible-only-with-a-spoon concoction called a Frosty.

This concludes our fast-food interlude; we now return to the regularly scheduled grammar-nerd crap.

MANDATORY Beware of redundancy when using this word, as in *D.C. law requires mandatory use of seat belts.* D.C. law requires use of seat belts. Use of seat belts is mandatory in the District of Columbia. But *requires mandatory use* is redundant, at least in this case, though it could make sense in a reference to a mandated mandate, as in *Federal highway-funding guidelines for the states require mandatory use of seat belts.*

MASSEUSE Not all massage therapists are masseuses. A masseuse, like an actress, must be *female*. A male massage therapist is a *masseur*.

MASTHEAD This is the box in a newspaper, usually found on the editorial page, that lists the publisher and top editors. The *flag*, or *nameplate*, is the strip with the logo and the price that you find at the top of Page One.

MATTRESS TAGS Remove one and you go to prison! Ha, ha!

Ahem. I'm not looking to send thousands of comedians to the unemployment line, but I feel duty-bound to report that those tags say they are not to be removed under penalty of law, *except by consumer*. I found this legal threat funny for the brief period between when I learned to read and when I learned what *consumer* means. (You hear that word a lot more today than you did in 1966, so even 5-year-olds should be hissing this comedy cliche.)

MAY, MIGHT There are those who would restrict the use of *may* to matters of permission:

> *Yes, you may go to the dance.*

I'm not a member of that camp. The language is full of synonyms, and you can't outlaw all of them. Sometimes *may* means the same thing as *might*, and there's nothing wrong with that. If there's some potential for confusion, of course, you can use *might* if you mean "maybe" and *may* if you mean "allowed to."

> *Johnny may go to the dance* (his mom said OK).
> *Johnny might go to the dance* (he hasn't decided yet).

MEANTIME, MEANWHILE Beginning sentences with *meantime* is a local-TV-news affectation that should be avoided in writing. Use *meanwhile*, not *meantime*, in the common adverbial construction (*Meanwhile, back at stately Wayne Manor . . .*). Use *meantime* only as a noun (*In the meantime . . .*).

MEETS, MEETINGS *Meet* should be confined to terms such as *track meet*. It is not acceptable as a headline substitute for *meeting*.

MET? HADN'T THEY ALREADY MET? *President Clinton met Syrian President Hafez Assad* means the two had never before made each other's acquaintance. If they're getting together for the second or third time, make it *met with*. In some constructions, of course, the distinction is moot—*Clinton, Assad Meet* is a perfectly good headline for either occasion.

MIKE A microphone, for short, is a *mike*, not a *mic*. Make it easy on the reader, who's bound to read the latter as "mick."

MILLENNIA The real word has two *n*'s, but the car—the Mazda Millenia—has just one, just as Coors leaves a *c* out of its Artic Ice beer. Call it clevver marketting.

MILLIONS AND BILLIONS *The project will cost between $2 and $3 million.* Two dollars to 3 million dollars? That's quite a range! Don't forget to repeat *million* in cases like this.

MINISTER Avoid using this term by itself when referring to a government official. While the term means Cabinet member in many countries, to many American readers it means clergyman. *Cabinet minister, foreign minister, transportation minister,* etc., are all OK, as is *minister* by itself on second reference if it's already established that the person is a government official and not a church official.

MINUSCULE A frequently misspelled word: It's not *miniscule*. Helpful hint: Think *minus*.

MOM AND DAD Capitalize such terms when they're used as substitute names: *Mom and Dad wouldn't let me stay up late.* Lowercase in other usages: *Jenna's mom and Jeremy's dad seemed to hit it off.*

MONIES That would be the plural of *mony*. Trouble is, *mony* isn't a word, unless you're thinking of Mutual of New York or that horribly overplayed rock-'n'-roll song. Just as the plural of *duh* is *duhs*, the plural of *money* is *moneys*.

No matter how you spell it, of course, this is an overused word (the simple collective *money* is quite versatile, and *funds* is at your disposal if you're dying to use a plural), but it is occasionally useful to emphasize that piles of funding came from various sources.

MORE-PERSUASIVE REASONS TO HYPHENATE Adjectival phrases starting with *more* are best left unhyphenated, but a hyphen is needed when the possibility of confusion exists. Does my book need *more relevant examples* (additional examples) or *more-relevant examples* (examples that are more relevant)?

MULTIPLE TITLES Drop capitalization of a title that would otherwise be capitalized when it's being strung together with another title (or a simple label) in front of a person's name: *Senate majority leader and GOP presidential candidate Bob Dole.*

MUSTACHE The preferred spelling in American English, not *moustache.*

MYRIAD Although *a myriad of things* is historically at least as correct as *myriad things*, the latter has emerged as the preferred choice among sophisticated writers and speakers. It's also shorter, of course, so it gets my vote.

NAMES OF TEAMS AND BANDS: SINGULAR OR PLURAL? Follow the usual rules of subject-verb agreement when confronted with one of those newfangled singular collective team names that seem to be especially popular in Florida. (Let's see, we have the Orlando Magic, the Miami Heat, the Tampa Bay Lightning, the non-Florida Colorado Avalanche and Utah Jazz, and too many teams to mention in the newer leagues, such as soccer and women's basketball.)

 WRONG: *The New Jersey Sludge are 7-0.*

RIGHT: *The New Jersey Sludge is 7-0.*

Yes, it sounds odd, but it sounds even more odd to trash logic in favor of consistency and make all teams plural. British English has an advantage over American English here, as the Brits treat all collective entities as plural (*New Jersey are 7-0*).

Band names work the same way:

The Beatles were great.
The Who was great.

NAMES: WHEN ONE SPOUSE HAS TWO The phrase *President and Hillary Rodham Clinton* implies there's a President Rodham Clinton. The following alternatives all are correct:

President and Hillary Clinton.
President Clinton and his wife, Hillary.
President Clinton and his wife, Hillary Rodham Clinton.
President Clinton and first lady Hillary Rodham Clinton.

NEAR MISSES, NEAR-MISSES AND NEAR-COLLISIONS A near miss is a hit, right?

Well, no.

A *near miss* is a miss that is near, just as a *red sweater* is a sweater that is red. Now, if you added a hyphen, you'd get a *near-miss*, nearly a miss, which is indeed a hit. In fact, it's best to avoid *near miss* and use the hyphenated *near-collision*—same meaning but clearer.

NERVE-RACKING Preferred to *nerve-wracking*. Likewise, you *rack* (not *wrack*) your brain.

NEWSSTAND Two *s*'s, no matter what your "roomate" says.

NO COMMENT? NO, COMMENT! *Kaputnik refused to comment on Mad magazine's allegations. "I will issue a statement through my lawyer next week on those scurrilous rumors," he said.*

It's surprising how often reporters introduce comments by denying there was any comment.

By the way, polite, impartial journalists write that someone *would not comment* or *declined to comment*; they avoid the loaded term *refused*.

A NON- ISSUE I'm in the minority on this issue, but I consider *non-* (like ANTI-) an in-between prefix—a prefix as opposed to a word, but not worthy of the automaticallymushedtogether treatment usually accorded such undeniably prefixy prefixes as *un-* and *over-*. With the exception of some well-established solid words that I will attempt to list, I think *non-* requires a hyphen—it is as much like the word *not* as it is like the prefix *un-*. It's jarring to present readers with a made-up-for-the-occasion word while pretending it's a longtime denizen of the literary landscape: If you were writing about the "mods" of 1960s London, would their sworn enemies, the "rockers," be *nonmods*?

I wish I could simply draw a distinction between custom-made *non-* words and off-the-rack ones, but the dictionary people have made the rack way too large. For example, Webster's New World lists *nonchurch* and *nonlife*. You might say I had a nonlife before I met my future wife, but otherwise I'm at a loss to find a use for such a word. Even the most anti-hyphen *non-* users would concede that *non-life-threatening* requires a hyphenated prefix—it means "not threatening to life," not "threatening to nonlife." Similarly, what in the world is a *nonchurch*? Is it something you would call any building that isn't a church, or is it intended as an adjective, as in *Church members should not attend nonchurch functions*? Even that doesn't make sense; such a sentence would refer to functions that are not church-related, not functions that are held at nonchurches.

Here are some *non-* words that I think can be used without a hyphen. This is not meant to be an exhaustive list, but take from it what you like. Note that many of them, in addition to being very common words, stray from the formula of *non-* meaning "not." *Nonchalant* and *nondescript* don't mean "not chalant" and "not descript." *Nonfat milk* doesn't mean "milk that is not fat"; it means "milk that is *without* fat." Subtle difference, but a difference all the same.

nonbeliever	*noncommittal*
nonbelieving	*noncompliance*
nonchalance	*nonconformist*
nonchalant	*nonconformity*
noncommissioned officer	*nondescript*

nonentity	*nonpartisan*
nonessential	*nonplus*
nonexistence	*nonplused*
nonexistent	*nonprofit*
nonfat	*nonrestrictive*
nonfeasance	*nonsense*
nonfiction	*nonsensical*
nonmember	*nonstandard*
nonpareil	*nonstop*

NON SEQUITURS Poorly constructed sentences can imply a causal relationship where none exists:

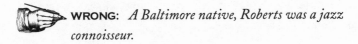 **WRONG:** *A Baltimore native, Roberts was a jazz connoisseur.*

Uh, is Baltimore a jazz mecca?

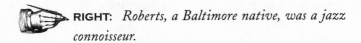 **RIGHT:** *Roberts, a Baltimore native, was a jazz connoisseur.*

It's fine to group unrelated details in one sentence, but one of the details should not act as an introductory clause. With related details, of course, all is well.

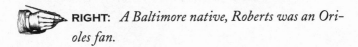 **RIGHT:** *A Baltimore native, Roberts was an Orioles fan.*

NO OBLIGATION TV ad writers probably don't make up a large portion of my readership, but if I'm mentioning such antiques as *icebox* and *c/o*, I have to include this phrase. It

obviously was included in early commercials to assuage the
fears of those who thought they were placing themselves in
financial peril by picking up a telephone in response to a television ad. Either in reality or in the Madison Avenue types'
imaginations, those people who were well into adulthood
when TV came on the scene feared that such newfangled
inventions as the moving-picture box and the talking machine
might be conspiring to electronically remove the money from
their wallets. (I shudder to think that the average American
was dumber in the 1950s than today, but then I reflect on the
panic that new technology continues to elicit in many otherwise well-adjusted adults and I understand.)

Anyway, my point here is that the "no obligation" phrase
has become a habit; if it ever made any sense, it certainly
makes none today.

NOON AND MIDNIGHT That's all—noon and midnight, not
12 noon or *12 midnight*, as if there's an 11 noon and an 11 midnight. And don't capitalize the words; they're not proper nouns.

NOR The word is often misused in place of *or*:

 WRONG: *People weren't buying stock in Microsoft, nor IBM.*

RIGHT: *People weren't buying stock in Microsoft
or IBM.*

Usually, *nor* requires a *neither*:

 RIGHT: *Neither dogs nor cats are allowed in the
apartment complex.*

RIGHT: *Agassi could defeat neither Sampras nor Kafelnikov in the round-robin exhibition.*

An exception to that rule occurs when *nor* begins a sentence or independent clause that follows another negative statement:

RIGHT: *Those attending the performance-art exhibition couldn't stomach Annie Sprinkle's act. Nor could they stand the guy pretending to be Mapplethorpe's corpse.*

RIGHT: *I wouldn't have painted the wall blue, nor would I have painted it green.*

BORDERLINE (BUT I'D CALL IT WRONG): *I will not paint the wall green, nor even a turquoise.*

RIGHT: *I will not paint the wall green, or even a turquoise.*

RIGHT: *I will not paint the wall green, nor will I choose a turquoise.*

Unlike *or* (or *and*), *nor* cannot act as a serial connector; it requires repetition after each element:

WRONG: *I would have painted the wall neither blue, green nor yellow.*

RIGHT: *I would have painted the wall neither blue nor green nor yellow.*

Finally, *nor* clauses are notorious for problems of paral-

lel construction. Both sides of the equation must be phrased
the same way:

 WRONG: *I will neither do it nor something else.*

RIGHT: *I will do neither it nor something else.*

RIGHT: *I will neither do it nor do something else.*

NUMBERS AND NUMERALS Newspaper style calls for spelling out one through nine and using numerals for 10 and up.
This includes numerals for the *1, 2*, etc., in *1 million, 2 billion*,
etc. It also includes ordinal numbers: *first, 10th, First Street,
10th Street*.

The beginning of a sentence is an exception, of course,
unless the number is a year:

Ten people showed up for the event.
Three hundred sixty-five days make up a year.
1977 was a very good year.

Make no exception, however, simply because a number is
part of a quotation. There is no difference in pronunciation
between *125* and *one hundred twenty-five*, and the former
should be used everywhere but at the beginning of a
sentence.

OFFICIOUS It's a shame the word doesn't mean what everybody thinks it means, because we really need such a word, and
this one sounds so right. What it *doesn't* mean is "overly official or overbearing in the exercise of one's authority," as in
*That officious bastard made a big show of reprimanding me in
front of the entire office.*

What it *does* mean is almost the opposite: "too attentive or eager to please," as in *That officious waiter asked us if everything was all right again!*

OK *Okay* doesn't bother me that much, but I think *OK* makes more sense, and it helped me write one of my favorite headlines: *FCC OKs WSEX.*

"ON" AS A BUFFER *Elsewhere in Yugoslavia Saturday . . .*

You mean the "Yugoslavia Saturday" promotion over at O'Hurlihey's Drinking Emporium? Spell *Balkanization* and get a 50-cent draft beer?

Make it *elsewhere in Yugoslavia on Saturday* or *elsewhere Saturday in Yugoslavia.* Grammar might not forbid back-to-back proper nouns, but aesthetics and ease of reading do. Reluctance to use *on* when it isn't absolutely necessary is a tenet of the same staccato school of writing and editing that all but bans the word THAT.

ON CONDITION *On condition of anonymity* is a phrase dear to the heart of every reporter, but it's grammatically flawed. Try *on the condition of anonymity.*

Also, avoid this sort of construction:

"President Clinton is a liar," he said on the condition of anonymity.

That kind of wording casts reporters in a bad light, as though they had a very specific idea of what they wanted a source to say and promised the source anonymity to get that specific quote. More accurately (one would hope), the reporter promised anonymity to get the source to talk, period. Try it this way:

"President Clinton is a liar," he said, speaking on the condition of anonymity.

ONE: DON'T TREAT THE ORIGINAL AS A SEQUEL There's no treaty called START I, just as there's no movie called "Rocky I." Except in quotes, or in a case where confusion is possible (I can't think of any such case offhand), call the treaties *START* and *START II*. *The first START pact* is another way of avoiding *START I.*

This reminds me of one of the old "Encyclopedia Brown" stories, the children's mysteries in which the readers have to figure out what's fishy and then check their answers against a solution at the end of the book. Someone was trying to sell a sword as a Civil War antique, and on it was engraved "First Battle of Bull Run." Encyclopedia Brown, junior detective, caught the scam, of course.

There was a similar howler in one of those horrible "Gilligan's Island" sequel movies (perhaps the one with the Harlem Globetrotters), in which the long-since-rescued castaways set off for the island on their new boat, the Minnow II, and landed on a beach where the first boat's wreckage still sat. Of course, "Minnow I" was painted on a plank from the hull.

THE "ONE OF THOSE" FALLACY Here's a tricky one (and, in my mind, a litmus test to sort out writers and editors who actually think and editors who memorize "rules" but lack the insight to tell when and how to apply them):

Gramm is one of many candidates for the GOP nomination who has come out against affirmative action.

Wrong. That *has* should be a *have*. Yes, I know that the singular *Gramm* is the subject of the sentence, but that doesn't matter. The subject of the *clause* is what matters, and that subject is *many candidates*.

This is one of those cases that are (*are*, not *is*) easier to explain through logic than through grammar: If you use *has*, all you're saying is that (a) Gramm is one of many candidates for the GOP nomination and (b) he has come out against affirmative action. The intent of the sentence, however, is to say that *many* candidates for the GOP nomination have come out against affirmative action, and that Gramm is one of them.

In other words, if the clause applies only to Gramm (and using *has* indicates that it does), what in the world are *many candidates* doing in the sentence?

Still not convinced? Take a look at this pair of sentences:

Gramm is one of the many GOP candidates who have come out against affirmative action. Specter is one of the few GOP candidates who have not come out against affirmative action.

Change *have* to *has* in both sentences, thereby making the statement about affirmative action apply only to the subject of each sentence, and you're saying (a) there are many GOP candidates and (b) there are few GOP candidates. The affirmative-action clause has to apply to the candidates (plural), and therefore it has to take a plural verb.

ONETIME, ONE-TIME Most style manuals rule one way or the other and be done with it, but I propose that we're dealing with two meanings that deserve different treatments.

One-time means just that: "one time": "*I slept with him,*" she said, "*but it was a one-time thing.*"

Onetime means "former": *The onetime Wall Street broker now lectures on the evils of greed.*

ON-LINE, ON LINE, ONLINE The term should generally be hyphenated: *on-line services, on-line chat.* But use two words in a sentence such as *I've been on line for five minutes now and I haven't found a thing.* The company America Online Inc. uses it as one word. See Chapter 3 for a discussion of the term's evolution.

"ON THE RISE" IS ON THE INCREASE! Reporters without anything more interesting to say about a subject tend to blindly assert that all issues of current interest involve trends that are "on the rise" or "on the increase." Be very careful about making such assertions. People who study child abductions, heroin use and other periodically recycled issues du jour will tell you that these claims are often wrong. Quote experts talking about an increase if you must, but keep in mind that unless they're citing actual statistics, they're quite possibly full of crap, too.

THE OP-ED PAGE It's the newspaper page *op*posite the *ed*itorial page, normally home to commentary articles from a variety of viewpoints. The *op* could very well stand for *opinion*, but it doesn't.

The meaning aside, this is newsroom jargon that should be reserved for newsroom use. Use *a commentary article* rather than *an op-ed article* when writing for a general-interest publication.

OVERHAND, OVERHEAD *Overhand* is an adjective that can describe a baseball or softball pitch, a punch in boxing, or a tennis stroke. *Overhead* is the noun that describes the tennis stroke also known as the *smash*.

OVER, MORE THAN This is one of those chestnuts that dabblers in the stylistic arts tend to pick as pet peeves. As with most of the others, it's more complicated than it seems.

Yes, with a number that represents a count of discrete entities, *more than* is preferable:

 WRONG: *Over 200 people attended the party.*

RIGHT: *More than 200 people attended the party.*

But when a number is, shall we say, more analog than digital, the objection to *over* becomes silly:

 RIGHT: *He was driving over 75 mph.*

RIGHT: *In just over 10 years, he made 22 movies.*

RIGHT: *His weight grew to over 300 pounds.*

RIGHT: *He was paid over a million dollars.*

When you're dealing with rates, as in miles per hour, or collective amounts, as with time, space and money, to use *more than* implies a one-unit-at-a-time ratcheting up, as if you're "counting" units that aren't meant to be counted that way. While the next step up from *200 people* is *201 people*, which is indeed "more than" 200, that's not quite the case with the other numbers, which rise either in much smaller units (pen-

nies) or in a gradual fashion for which our measurements are
only arbitrary (how many decimal places down do you want
to go to express the tiniest bit over 75 mph or 10 years or 300
pounds?). My preference for *over* in these cases is simply a
matter of style, you might say, but I think it can also be a matter of correctness. I would argue that to travel "more than 75"
miles per hour, you'd have to get to 76. *More than 10 years*
doesn't cover 10 years and a month, *more than 300 pounds*
doesn't cover 300.5 pounds, and *more than a million dollars*
doesn't cover $1,000,000.99.

All of this, of course, also applies to *under* vs. *less than*.

PABLUM Once upon a time, people actually used the word
pabulum, which means "nourishment." Some bright marketing
type seized on this and came up with the name *Pablum* for a
gruel of some sort (once upon a time, people actually used the
word *gruel*). The blandness of the capital-*P Pablum* led to the
small-*p pablum*, which means "bland thought or writing." In
a way, then, *pabulum*, as something substantial, is the opposite
of *pablum*, so watch that extra *u*.

PARALLEL CONSTRUCTION A TV news report said:

> *There are reports that the boy was beaten, molested and is*
> *now a drug addict.*

That's a classic non-parallel construction. It's clear what
the anchorwoman was trying to say, but she didn't succeed.
The words could be read two ways, and neither makes sense:

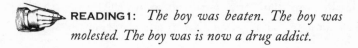 **READING 1:** *The boy was beaten. The boy was*
molested. The boy was is now a drug addict.

READING 2: *The boy was beaten. The boy molested. The boy is now a drug addict.*

Was is now a drug addict? *The boy molested*? Either *was* applies to each item in the series or it applies only to the first one, the one it was directly attached to. You can't have it both ways; you can't have it apply to a bunch of items in the series and then change the rules in the middle. There are usually two ways to fix a problem like this, and the first one is no doubt resisted by many because they think *and* can't occur more than once in a sentence:

The boy was beaten and molested and is now a drug addict.

The other method also involves some repetition. People are lazy, and that would explain why most of them would rather mutilate the language than repeat the word *was*:

The boy was beaten, was molested and is now a drug addict.

PEOPLE, PERSONS The AP stylebook wisely advises the use of *people* in all instances. "The Elements of Style" (aka Strunk and White) argues that *persons* should be the plural of choice when an exact number is involved, with *people* reserved for broad, sweeping statements (*Hundreds of people crashed the gates*). Mr. Strunk argues: *If of "six people" five went away, how many people would be left? Answer: one people.*

With all due respect, I say that's a flawed argument. You can't outlaw irregular plurals. If one sheep is joined by another, do we need to say there are now *two sheeps*?

PERCENT It hasn't been *per cent* since, like, 1940 or something. Unless you're at the New Yorker.

PERIODICAL NAMES The names of newspapers, magazines and journals, no matter what language they're in, never take quotation marks: the Washington Post, Newsweek, Pravda, Sports Illustrated. Some publications italicize them; others (as I do) use regular roman type. (Book titles, with the exception of reference works, go in quotes in newspaper style—"For Whom the Bell Tolls," "Crime and Punishment," "Profiles in Courage," the Encyclopaedia Britannica—but all book titles are generally italicized in non-newspaper writing.)

If your publication chooses, italics may be used for periodical names, but this is not a valid style recommendation across the board, because wire services cannot transmit the coding for italics and many newspapers lack the typeface flexibility to use them. Rule of thumb: Titles take quotes; names don't. Newspapers and magazines have names, while movies and TV shows have titles.

Occasionally you'll run into a periodical with a colon in the middle of the title; in such a case, if you're not using italics, the colon assumes an unwanted role as a participant in the entire sentence. To avoid this, phrase the first reference in such a way that justifies quote marks. *Called* is an excellent tool for this:

> *Steinem's remarks appeared in a new journal called "Les Femmes: The Women of Truth."*

Then, on subsequent references, *Les Femmes* can be used alone, without the subtitle and without the quotes.

The that is either present or implied in most newspaper names, combined with the italic-vs.-roman issue, creates special problems when newspapers refer to other newspapers. Some newspapers use italics in such citations, while others stick with just the capital letters. Either is fine, but I prefer the latter. Still other newspapers, no doubt, use quotation marks, and this must be considered an error, since newspapers have names, not titles. (Many papers that use italics for newspaper names in text switch to quotation marks for them in headlines; again, I think this is wrong. And italics should not be used in the middle of a non-italic headline; it looks goofy.) The only real option in headlines is plain, capitalized text.

The other controversy is whether to follow a publication's preference on capitalization of *the*. I prefer not to, because (a) it's usually an affectation and (b) it means you have to keep looking in the Editor & Publisher Yearbook to see whether this newspaper or that uses the *The*.

Many newspapers' names do not contain the city in which they are published. And newspapers published in small cities often need the state or country inserted so that readers know where exactly they are. Proper style for such insertions depends on whether your publication uses italics and whether it capitalizes the *The*. London's most respected newspaper, for example, is The Times. It is not, contrary to popular belief, called The Times of London; that construction is derived from one of the correct ways of specifying the city (as follows). Let's take a look at how you'd handle The Times and The Tampa Tribune with the various style alternatives.

If you use *The* and italics, it's best not to break up italicized names with a roman insertion, so use this form:

The Times of London
The Tampa Tribune in Florida

If you use *The* and no italics:

The (London) Times
The Tampa (Fla.) Tribune

If you use *the* and italics:

the London *Times*
the *Tampa Tribune* in Florida

If you use neither *the* nor italics:

the London Times
the Tampa Tribune in Florida

If you lowercase the *The* and skip the italics, it creates a problem with certain publications, such as The European and The Hill, which are difficult to identify as newspapers when you strip away both extra clues. It's not a great solution, but here's how I handle the problem:

According to the Capitol Hill newspaper the Hill, . . .

If you lowercase the *The*, you should also generally delete it from a newspaper's name in strictly label-style uses, such as bylines (otherwise, you're back to having to look such things up). Again, however, this can be a problem. It looks silly to use:

By JOHN SMITH
European

Papers that choose to drop the italics and lowercase the *t*'s might be best advised to create ad hoc exceptions for these rare cases. Another exception that should be granted to the lowercase-*t* rule is when the *The* actually means something in a publication name. Imagine a magazine called The Meaning of Life or The Whole Story—take out the *The* and the name makes no sense.

PLACEBO EFFECTS Maybe I'm reading too much into the *placebo (sugar pill)* notation that we see over and over and over in the medical literature that has become an advertising staple, but I fear that people are taking this "definition" at face value. The word *placebo* does not *mean* "sugar pill." A sugar pill is a widely used placebo, but a placebo—an inert agent that is perceived as an effective agent—can be a variety of things. A whispered phrase or a cue card could act as one in certain tests.

The TV commercials commit the same error (in addition to a grammatical error) when they say a drug's side effects were "similar to sugar pill." It's the placebo effect, not the sugar pill itself, that causes headaches, dry mouth and nausea.

PLAYBOY: PLAYMATES, CENTERFOLDS, BUNNIES, MODELS AND MERE POSERS Playboy magazine's resonance in pop culture presents a host of opportunities for confusion in print. Despite what appears in the popular press, not every woman who doffs her clothing for the publication is a Bunny or a Playmate or even a "Playboy model."

A *Playboy Bunny* (note capitalization), with the celebrated cottontail uniform, is a waitress at a Playboy Club. The species is now extinct; the last Playboy Club closed in 1991.

Playmate and *centerfold* are synonymous. There is a Playmate of the Month in each issue, and she is the one who graces the centerfold and several surrounding pages. One of every year's 12 Playmates is chosen as Playmate of the Year. Note that there are no "former Playmates"; once a Playmate, always a Playmate (note capitalization).

Playboy model is a tricky term. Generically it would seem to be an acceptable reference to anyone who poses in the magazine, but one part of the Playboy empire is (or at least was) a modeling agency, and therefore *Playboy model* suggests a different meaning. For the sake of clarity, references to women

I'M A MEMBER OF THE MEDIA, BUT I'M NOT A MEDIUM

"Media" Isn't Always Plural, No Matter What You've Been Taught

Media used as a plural means "more than one medium." Fine. If you're using the word as a plural, make it plural: *Representatives of all of the news media attended the conference.*

But that's not usually the way it's used nowadays. In a reference to *the media gathered outside the courthouse*, the word is used as a synonym for *press*, as a collective noun meaning "the representatives of each medium." Still a plural, you say? Well, yes, it's a plural of *media representatives* or *media outlets*, but it's not a plural of *medium*. Each individual unit of "the media" in this sense is a reporter or photographer or newspaper or magazine; unlike with the legitimate plural, the units are not "TV," "radio" and "print."

Substitute *mediums* for *media* and see if any contemporary uses of the term make any sense: *The mediums are biased?* Uh-uh. People who say the media is biased mean there's an inherent bias in Dan Rather and Ted Koppel and Peter Jennings. They don't mean there's an inherent bias in TV cameras, radio microphones and printing presses.

As with the popular use of HOPEFULLY, of course, it takes guts to publish *the media is* and risk incurring the wrath of educated but misguided readers. It would be nice if we could use footnotes.[1]

---

[1] You may think this is a usage error. It isn't, and here's why . . .

who posed in Playboy but weren't Playmates should avoid the shorthand and say something like *women who posed in Playboy.*

PLEADED, PLED The past tense of *plead* is *pleaded*, not *pled.*

PLURALS Some irregular plurals are mandatory (it's *sheep*, not *sheeps*), but others are optional. If your dictionary lists a regular option, use it: *cactuses*, not *cacti*; *indexes*, not *indices.*

PLURALS OF PROPER NOUNS These generally follow the same rules as other plurals, but take care not to change the spelling of the proper noun in question—for example, it's *Grammys*, not *Grammies*. Note also that, despite the time-honored apostrophe style used by folks with woodburning kits who create signs for people's mailboxes and garages, the standard *-s* or *-es* plural applies to family names, even those that end with the letter *s*. So the Reynolds family is *the Reynoldses*, the Walsh family is *the Walshes*, and so on. "The Simpsons" occasionally portrays a ridiculous-sounding Homer calling the Flanders family next door "the Flanderses," but he's absolutely correct. And if you're implying a possessive, as in *Come on over to the Flanderses' for milk and cookies*, use the apostrophe. *The Flanderses'* is short for *the Flanderses' house*.

Then there's the issue of plurals of *possessive* proper nouns. There's no good way to refer to more than one McDonald's or more than one Denny's, but try to avoid using a possessive name as a plural, as in *Two McDonald's were opened yesterday at the South Pole*. Instead, try *McDonald's restaurants* or *McDonald's outlets* or *McDonald's locations*.

POLICE *Detroit Police Department*, for example, and the shortened form *Police Department* should be capitalized, assuming that's the department's formal name, but *police* is lowercase in *Detroit police, Houston police, Sarajevo police*, etc.

POSSESSIVES OF POSSESSIVES As with plurals of possessives, there's no easy answer. *I love McDonald's fries* could be read as a possessive, as loving the fries of McDonald (incorrect), or as a simple label, loving the fries that are *McDonald's fries* (just fine). So you're safe there. *I love McDonald's employee benefits* works the same way. But *I love McDonald's training program* makes no sense unless the place running the program is simply called *McDonald*. The difference is that the latter sentence requires a *the*; you could legitimately say *I love employee benefits*, but you couldn't say *I love training program*, unless you're Tonto. Similarly, observe the following, taken from a genuine tub of Lloyd's barbecue pork: *Lloyd's tub is microwaveable*. So who the heck is Lloyd? The meat may belong to Lloyd, but the tub belongs to *Lloyd's*. When confronted with a case like this, the easiest solution is to stick in that *the*, as in *the Lloyd's tub*. You can write *I love the McDonald's training program*, but you can't very well write *I love McDonald's's training program*.

PRESCHOOL, PRE-SCHOOL A *preschool* is a place where children too young for kindergarten receive day care and some education. *Pre-school* is an adjective that means "before school." Consider the difference between *preschool-age children* (children old enough to go to preschool but not old enough to go to school) and *pre-school-age children* (which includes newborns).

PRESCRIBE, PROSCRIBE A guidebook reported the following about my home city, the District of Columbia:

> *"It's very safe," says Officer Rod Ryan of D.C.'s Metropolitan Police Department, as long as you stay in proscribed areas.*

The writer's paraphrase mangled the policeman's point. To *prescribe* is to "recommend"; to *proscribe* is "to condemn or forbid."

PRESENTLY The traditional meaning is "in a short while": *I will be there presently*. Avoid using it as a synonym for *currently*. (This should not be interpreted as prohibiting the use of *present* as a synonym for *current*.)

RETRONYMS, OR SOMETIMES A MUFFIN IS JUST A MUFFIN

Technology's March Adds Clarifying Adjectives to Formerly Clear Terms

I had been pondering this phenomenon for a few years when I came across the word *retronym* in a William Safire column. The term, coined by former Robert Kennedy aide and National Public Radio president Frank Mankiewicz, refers to the addition to a word of a qualifier that once would have seemed painfully redundant. Think of *snow skiing*, *ice skating*, *acoustic guitar* and *postal mail*—terms that came about through the advent of waterskiing, roller skating, electric guitars and electronic mail. Mankiewicz says he came up with the word after hearing a reference to *natural turf* on a TV football telecast.

Sometimes these qualifiers are necessary (*roller* is giving *ice* a run for its money in the

world of skating), and sometimes they're necessary in a certain context (*snow skiing* in Florida
or *acoustic guitar* in a rock-'n'-roll publication),
but often they're gratuitous and annoying.

Mail doesn't mean "postal mail" to you in a
non-AOL-start-up-screen situation? Say *gin
martini* in front of me an you'd think I was on
the Tanqueray payroll. And I don't mean to be
morbid, but what is the deal with *non-Hodgkin's
lymphoma*? Hodgkin's disease is a form of lymphoma? Fine. I understand that. But if I meant
Hodgkin's disease, I'd say Hodgkin's disease. So
why isn't regular old lymphoma called *lymphoma*?

There are retronyms and there are retronyms—at least water skiing doesn't involve
snow. In a misguided search for parallelism,
though, writers (usually advertising copywriters)
often misleadingly highlight some irrelevant
detail that is by no means unique to the item at
hand. Instead of *milk* or even *regular milk* alongside the fat-free milk and the chocolate milk, we
get *vitamin D* milk or *homo* milk, as if fat-free
and chocolate milk aren't homogenized or rich in
vitamin D. A 7-Eleven commercial advertises
"*frozen* cappuccino or *mocha* cappuccino," even
though the mocha version is every bit as frozen
as the non-mocha version. Then there's *cheese*

continued

pizza, as opposed to *pepperoni pizza.* You get the picture.

A coffeehouse I used to frequent offered both muffins and English muffins. You're with me so far, right? You know what a muffin is? At this place, however, I'd ask for a blueberry muffin and the server would always ask, "English muffin or country muffin?" *Country muffin?* Never mind that that's not an actual term: Would *anybody* who wanted an English muffin ask for "a muffin"? That would be like referring to table tennis as "tennis."

PROFESSOR Capitalize only when it's used as a formal title before a name *and* it's not modified by a subject. And be sure it's a correct formal title: It's perfectly OK to call an assistant professor *professor,* but once you capitalize it, it becomes an error.

> *I asked Professor Harvey Baxter for his opinion.* (Baxter is a full professor.)

> *I asked professor Harvey Baxter for his opinion.* (He's not a full professor, but his exact standing isn't important to the story.)

> *I asked philosophy professor Harvey Baxter for his opinion.* (Baxter may or may not be a full professor, but the title must be lowercased if accompanied by a discipline.)

I asked Assistant Professor Harvey Baxter for his opinion. (Here we have a formal title.)

I asked Harvey Baxter, an assistant professor of philosophy, for his opinion. (Always recast the sentence when you want to use both a complex formal title and a discipline.)

Note also: For some reason, people tend to write things like *Harvey Baxter is professor of philosophy at Pima College.* Nobody *is professor.* He's *a professor.* If he's the only one, you can make it *the professor.* (If he's living with Juliet Mills, you can make it *Nanny and the Professor.*)

PROPER NAMES THAT AREN'T: PHOENIX AIRPORT Proper names often work just fine without an article:

The plane landed at Sky Harbor International Airport.

Many writers try to carry over this article-free construction to ad hoc constructions that imitate proper nouns but decidedly aren't:

The plane landed at Phoenix airport.

It's *the Phoenix airport* or *Phoenix's airport* but never Phoenix airport. It'd be different if it were Phoenix Airport, but that's not the name.

PROPHECY, PROPHESY *Prophecy* is a noun; *prophesy* is a verb, one meaning of which is "to make a prophecy."

PROSTATE, PROSTRATE The gland is the *prostate; prostrate* means "lying face down."

PSEUDO-CORPORATE ENTITIES School systems, political campaigns and the like might function as companies in some real sense, but their names should be treated as simple lowercase descriptions. Use *the Gore campaign* or *Al Gore's presidential campaign*, not the uppercased *Gore for President*. Use *the Montgomery County school system*, not the uppercased *Montgomery County Schools*.

PUBLICLY Not *publically*.

RANKINGS Sports fans (now I'm starting to sound like the Great Santini) will recognize this sort of silly but all-too-common error:

> *No. 3 Florida State is the lowest-ranked team to lose to North Carolina State this year.*

> *Agassi seldom loses to players ranked as high as No. 165 Doug Flach.*

Um, OK: The numbers 1 and 2 and 3 are indeed *lower* than the numbers 24 and 165 and 3,768. But high and low *rankings* are references to the relative loftiness of the *rankings*, not the *numbers*. No. 1 is *higher* than any other ranking. If you can't understand this, Robert Duvall and I will be glad to slap you around.

RBI, RBIs The style of many a sports page is to make *RBI* the plural of *RBI*: *He had three RBI.*

Three RBI? Is that like *three POW*? It's silly, if well intentioned, to try to apply this kind of internal logic once you've switched from a spelled-out term to an initialism. The plural of an initialism is the initialism plus *s*. *Prisoner of war/prisoners of war*, but *POW/POWs*. *Run batted in/runs bat-ted in*, but *RBI/RBIs*.

RECREATIONAL EDITING To *recreate* is to "have fun." To "create again" is to *re-create*. Although the prefix *re-* usually goes hyphenless, the hyphen should always be used if an unre-lated word would otherwise be produced. The U.S. Treasury periodically *re-funds*, as opposed to refunding. A gang might *re-form* even if it doesn't *reform*. A newspaper article typeset and pasted up (laid down) the old-fashioned way might have to *re-lay* for later editions, a concept that has nothing to do with the word *relay*. And, of course, there always lurks the possibility of a humorous but nasty misunderstanding when you inform someone that you sent something again by writ-ing *I resent that*.

REDUNDANCIES *ATM machine. ABM missile. HIV virus. START treaty. PIN number.*

In each of these oft-used terms, the word that follows the initialism repeats the word that the final initial stands for. We can't have this.

REESE'S MONKEYS Unless they're chocolate on the outside and peanut butter on the inside, you probably mean *Rhesus monkeys*.

RENOWNED If you want to say David Copperfield is a world-renowned magician, that's how to say it. A person with renown is *renowned*, not *renown* or the oddly popular *reknown*.

REVEREND *Reverend* occupies a unique place in the world of usage. It's not really a title (it's an adjective), but practically everyone uses it as a title. Think of it this way: Just as Judge John Smith might be called *the honorable John Smith*, clergyman John Smith is known as *the reverend John Smith*. The difference is that *reverend* is capped and abbreviated and mandatory: *the Rev. John Smith*.

Points to remember:

- Don't forget the *the* before *Rev.*

- To call someone *a reverend* is nonsense, just as it would be nonsense to call a judge *an honorable*.

A RIGHT HOOK Screenwriters and advertising copywriters are overly enamored of this punch in the boxer's arsenal. Yes, the punch does exist, but it's not exactly a staple, except among the minority of fighters who are left-handed. Right-handed boxers generally throw left jabs, left hooks and right crosses, along with the occasional left or right uppercut.

RISES AND FALLS *Amalgamated stock rose $2 to $10 a share.*

Does this mean the shares rose by somewhere between $2 and $10, or does it mean they started at $8 and rose to $10? A comma is in order:

Amalgamated stock rose $2, to $10 a share.

RISE UP! FALL DOWN! Here's another error that, as the reporters like to say about everything, is "on the rise":

Amalgamated stock rose to $10 a share, up from $2.

As opposed to rising to $10, *down* from $2.

ROOMMATE Two *m*'s, unless you ate a room or mated with a roo.

PASSIVE AGGRESSION

The Active Voice Is Overrated

Oops. I guess those who disagree would make that *People Overrate the Active Voice.*

See what I mean? Sometimes the object of a sentence is more important than the subject. Sometimes the subject is so obvious as to be utterly uninteresting. If I want to report that the Powerball numbers will be drawn tonight, what would be the point of assigning that action to someone? "A lottery official will draw the Powerball numbers tonight"? "Herbert J. Melton, 42, will draw the Powerball numbers tonight"?

Now, don't get me wrong. I said *overrated*, not *always inferior*. Most of the time, "Use the active voice" is good advice.

THE RUN-DOWN RUNDOWN *Rundown* is one word when referring to a summary: *He gave me the rundown on the situation*. But it's hyphenated as an adjective meaning "shabby": *The Washington Times is in a run-down area of town*. As a verb, of course, it's two words: *The officer tried to run down the suspect*.

SAVAGE BREAST No, it's not *savage beast*. The Congreve line goes like this: "Music has charms to soothe a savage breast, to soften rocks, or bend a knotted oak."

SCHIZOPHRENIC *Schizophrenia* is a psychiatric term for a complex condition unrelated to multiple-personality disorder. Thus it's inaccurate, even in a playful reference, to describe an indecisive or inconsistent person as schizophrenic.

SCORES AND COMMAS AP style calls for no comma before sports scores: *The Tigers beat the Orioles 3-1*. Some publications use the comma: *The Yankees beat the Royals, 10-2*. It's tempting to adopt a one-size-fits-all rule on such style matters—and in this case, most publications take the autopilot route—but neither of these style choices can be applied across the board in literate writing.

The preceding examples work either way, depending on a publication's style. But once you go beyond simple constructions and simple verbs (*beat, defeated, topped, lost to, fell to*), a comma becomes necessary. This is most apparent in headlines, where attention-grabbing language often makes the score an afterthought (and therefore a nonessential—comma required—element):

Cubs Sosa-rific Over Padres 7-3.

Uh, no. The Cubs might have been "Sosa-rific," and they might have defeated the Padres 7-3, but it makes no sense to talk of "being Sosa-rific 7-3." Use the comma.

Using the comma in all cases can be even worse:

Despite being behind, 21-3, Notre Dame rallied to win the game.

Preceeding the 21-3 score with a comma makes the score a nonessential element. That comma implies that the only notable thing about Notre Dame's comeback was the fact that it was a comeback. If the point of the sentence was that the Fighting Irish came a *long* way back—that overcoming an 18-point deficit is more impressive than overcoming a 1-point deficit—that comma has to be benched.

SCORES AND TALLIES: FIRST THINGS FIRST Just as you don't say the Orioles lost 1-4, don't say a bill was defeated 181-242 (or whatever). The reversed construction is applicable to indicate sets or games won by the loser in multiple-set (or multiple-game) sports such as tennis, badminton, squash and volleyball, but again you never reverse the entire score based on whether you're saying *won* or *lost*:

Gerulaitis thrilled the crowd in that 1977 Wimbledon semi-final, but he lost to Borg, 6-3, 3-6, 6-4, 3-6, 8-6.

SENTENCE FRAGMENTS Many good writers use fragments. Bad writers use them too, so it's a judgment call, but only the most tin-eared, fuddy-duddy excuses for copy editors routinely convert every single fragment they see into a complete sentence.

SEQUENCE OF TENSES: HE SAID IT WAS QUESTIONABLE I prefer to use logic, not strictly formal grammar, as a guide when dealing with sequence-of-tenses problems. British writers in particular tend to put everything in the past tense if it follows a past-tense attribution: *He said two plus two equaled four.* Assuming that the speaker isn't implying his statement is no longer true, I use the present tense: *He said two plus two equals four.* The British example isn't likely to cause confusion, but often there is that possibility: *The pope said the Catholic Church was against homosexual marriage.* (Isn't the church still against it?)

At least British English is consistent. My problem with the use of the sequence of tenses by American writers is that it is so haphazard. Sometimes you see it; sometimes you don't. I prefer to drop the pretense, so to speak, and dispense with it whenever possible.

SHAKING YOUR HEAD *Shaking one's head* means "no." The "yes" head movement is called a *nod.* Thus a person cannot "shake her head yes."

SHARING THE SAME *They share the same birthday—July 14.* As opposed to sharing a different birthday? *Sharing the same* can always be changed to *having the same* or simply *sharing.*

SHEETROCK It's a brand name. Use *plasterboard* or another generic equivalent; if *Sheetrock* appears in a quote, capitalize it.

SHUE, ELISABETH The actress is *Elisabeth Shue*—that's an *s*, not a *z*, in her first name.

SIDE Say *side order* or *side dish* if that's what you mean. *A side of coleslaw* isn't hurting anybody, but the naked generic use of the shortened form ("Three pieces of chicken plus two sides!") is quite grating.

"SIMILIAR": THE ALL-TIME TYPO CHAMP *Similiar*. Rhymes with *familiar*. A large percentage of attempts to type the word *similar* turn out this way. (Thanks to Frank Miele, my very first copy chief, for warning me about this phenomenon.)

SINCE I'm not here to complain about its being misused in place of *because*; unless there's a possibility of confusion regarding the time element, that's perfectly fine except in the most formal writing.

What I am concerned about is the following kind of misuse:

> *Today's high temperature was 101 degrees, the highest for this date since 1913, when the mercury rose to 99.*

It might seem like an obvious point, but this is a pretty common error. For 101 to be the highest temperature *since* 1913, the temperature in 1913 has to have been equal to or higher than 101.

SINGULAR VS. PLURAL WHEN NOUNS BECOME MODIFIERS
How many Cub fans in a Teamster election? Well, none. The question of singular vs. plural when a noun becomes a modifier is a sticky one, but it's best to let proper nouns retain any plural characteristics they may have. Thus a fan of the Cubs is a *Cubs fan*. When the Teamsters have an election, it's a *Teamsters election*. (The desire to drop these *s*'s is a strong one,

and I wouldn't be at all surprised to read about *Burt Reynold movies*.)

With common nouns, the general rule is to go with the singular, which is why we have *burger joints* and *cocktail lounges* that serve multiple burgers and cocktails. That tradition doesn't always hold. Note that *weapons* remains plural in *weapons depot* and *women* remains plural in *women senators* (which really should be *female* senators, but that's another issue, discussed in the FEMALE, WOMEN entry). I suppose you could get pedantic and insist on *weapon depots*, but you'd still have to bow to the weight of common usage (and common sense) before stooping to *arm control*.

SIR? NO SIR! People are people, knighted or not. Unless you're writing for the Fairy-Pixie Gazette, official newspaper of Ye Olde Sioux Falls Renaissance Faire, a knighted John Smith is *Smith* on second reference, not *Sir John*.

SIX-PACKS, NINE-IRONS AND THE EIGHT-BALL Number-plus-word nouns generally take the hyphen, a convention that makes it clear the writer isn't referring to six of them there packs or nine of them there irons.

-SIZE It's *small and medium-size*, with no hyphen after *small*, not *small- and medium-size* (you say "small," not "small-size"; *small* and *large* inherently refer to size, whereas *medium* does not). To imply *small-size* is analogous to writing of a SLOW-SPEED CHASE.

SKEPTIC, SKEPTICAL, SKEPTICISM In Britain they're sceptics. In the United States, we use the *k*.

SLOW-SPEED CHASE? The O.J. Simpson freeway parade was a low-speed chase, not a slow-speed chase. The concept of speed is inherent in the words *slow* and *fast*, so something is either slow or low-speed, either fast or high-speed. Other examples of this kind of redundancy include *delicious taste, hot temperatures* and *beautiful-looking*.

SMITHSONIAN The famed group of museums in Washington, D.C., is the *Smithsonian Institution*, not the *Smithsonian Institute* (I heard the latter mistake twice in one hour on two different cable-TV travel shows). Note the word *group*—there is no single museum called *the Smithsonian*.

SMOOTH The adjective and the verb are spelled the same way. Many writers, no doubt confused by *soothe*, write *smoothe* for the verb.

SO-CALLED The phrase carries the connotation of phoniness or incompetence ("Your so-called lawyer doesn't even have a bachelor's degree!"). So avoid using it to state the obvious—if you tell readers that something or someone is called something, you don't need to add those words. If a term is unfamiliar, you can always use quotation marks.

 WRONG: *Judge Lance Ito appointed a so-called special master to handle the mysterious envelope.*

RIGHT: *Judge Lance Ito appointed a "special master" to handle the mysterious envelope.*

SOFT-PEDAL To "tone down a point" is to *soft-pedal* it. *Soft-peddle* might work as a pun if you're referring to a *soft* *sell*, but any other use of that spelling must be considered an error.

Spock and Spock Dr. Spock is the pediatrician and author. Mr. Spock is the "Star Trek" character. (I've never actually seen an entire episode of the show, but I know that much.)

SPORT-UTILITY VEHICLES The term should be hyphenated (despite what Webster's New World says), but not for the reason you might think. It's not that *sport utility* is a compound modifier, the way *all terrain* is in *all-terrain vehicle*. With *sport-utility vehicle*, the hyphen gives equal weight to two modifiers, each of which is integral to the object's identity. It's like *indoor-outdoor carpeting*. SUVs (an acceptable term on second reference) are most aptly described as *vehicles that combine sport and utility*.

If you deleted the hyphen, you'd have *utility vehicles characterized by sport*. That might sound right too, but it's not what the term was intended to mean. If you used a comma (*sport, utility vehicles*), you'd have *vehicles that are both sport and utility*. The description seems to meet my criteria, but the comma construction is more suited to ad hoc descriptions than to permanent terms of identity, and the modifiers being used in this case are not true adjectives, although they play the role when they're put in that position. It's hard to imagine the following conversation:

> *"That vehicle sure is sport!"*
> *"Yes! And did you notice it's also utility?"*

The truncated noun *sport-utility* should be avoided, but you might come across it in a quote. It should also take a hyphen, to make it clear that the noun is being formed by two adjectives. Without the hyphen, it looks as if the adjective *sport* is describing the noun *utility*. This hyphen sometimes goes by the wayside when the truncated form takes on a life of its own (*hash browns*), but that hasn't happened here.

STANDARD SHIFT I'm not against all idioms, mind you, but the practice of referring to a manual transmission in a car as "a standard" really strips my gears. If you're talking about a four-speed or a five-speed or a stick shift or a manual transmission, say it. The fact that such a transmission is standard equipment, that you have to pay extra to get an automatic transmission, usually isn't the most important feature of such a transmission. (And these days the "standard" part isn't necessarily even true. Plenty of cars come with automatic transmission at no extra cost—"Can you drive a standard?" could just as easily mean "Can you drive a car without a CD player?")

Besides, when I hear talk of a standard transmission, I usually think of the three-on-the-tree that came as standard equipment on the Biscayne, Bel Air and Impala back in Chevy's heyday. I don't know if GM even manufactured such a transmission after 1968 or so; I think buyers automatically kicked in the few hundred extra to get the treasured P-R-N-D-L instead of the dreaded 1-2-3-N-R.

"STAR WARS" Midway through 1999, in perhaps the largest outbreak of mass stupidity since the world decided that *email* was a word, people and publications were gushing about this new movie—"Star Wars."

Uh, "Star Wars" is an *old* movie, released in 1977. It's one of the most recognizable titles in movie history. Heck, it was *re*-released, *amid great fanfare*, in 1997. Did people somehow forget all that?

There *was* in 1999 a new movie in the series it spawned, and I realize that "Star Wars, Episode I: The Phantom Menace" is a pain to fit into headlines, but while it's one thing to refer to *the "Star Wars" prequel* or *the new "Star Wars" movie* or even simply *the "Star Wars" movie*, with "you know, the one everybody's currently talking about" implied and understood, it's quite another to blather on about "Star Wars," which is only slightly closer to correct than calling this new movie "Duck Soup" or "Citizen Kane."

And please, spare me the "Episode IV: A New Hope" nonsense. The annotated title is irrelevant: Plain old naked "Star Wars" means the movie that was actually called "Star Wars."

STATE ABBREVIATIONS In actual writing, states should be abbreviated only when accompanied with a city, and then only using the traditional abbreviations, which you will find in the AP stylebook:

> *Seven travelers from Minnesota stopped in Kansas City, Mo., on their way to Shamrock, Texas.*

AP style does not allow for the use of postal abbreviations, but I would make an exception when citing a full address:

> *Contributions may be sent to P.O. Box 714, Madison Heights, MI 48071.*

STATED Lots of editors change *said* to *stated* when the "speaker" is a document and not a person, under the theory that only people, not things, can "say." I don't get it. If a document can't "say," it can't "state" either. This book *says* plenty of things, and among them is that inanimate objects can speak volumes. "Stated" isn't wrong, but it isn't necessary.

STATES Be careful when reporting state-by-state information that includes the District of Columbia. The District is not a state, so the word *jurisdiction* comes to the forefront in such cases:

> *In a survey of 50 states and the District of Columbia, all of the jurisdictions reported a drop in crime.*

STOCK PRICES If a stock rises 2 points, that means $2, and if it rises one-eighth, that means an eighth of a dollar, or 12½ cents. Most people probably know that, especially with the recent surge of ordinary-person stock investing, but writers should skip Wall Street's "points" and fractions and talk dollars and cents to educate those who don't know.

STOMACH Use *abdomen* for general references to the mid-section. *He was shot in the stomach* is fine if the bullet indeed entered the food-repository organ, but normally that's not what people mean when they say that.

SUBCOMMITTEES It's sloppy to mention a subcommittee without naming the committee it belongs to.

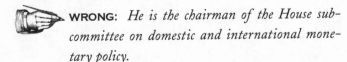

WRONG: *He is the chairman of the House subcommittee on domestic and international monetary policy.*

RIGHT: *He is the chairman of the House Banking and Financial Services subcommittee on domestic and international monetary policy.*

Note the common convention of lowercasing subcommittee names and appending them to committee names without using the word *committee*. A more formal approach would be an equally valid style decision:

He is the chairman of the House Banking and Financial Services Committee's Domestic and International Monetary Policy Subcommittee.

"SUBSTANCE" ABUSE The term *substance abuse* is a handy catchall that avoids the possibility of leaving something out as humans get more creative in their efforts to chemically escape reality. Whatever it is that Americans are smoking, it's powerful stuff—powerful enough to induce collective amnesia. People don't seem to remember that the word *substance* existed long before the term *substance abuse*, and so we now have *substance-free dorms*, built, presumably, out of Zen consciousness.

SUPER It can be an adjective or a prefix, aside from the prefix you see in words such as *superstructure*. The difference is subtle, but, as Justice Potter Stewart said, I know it when I see it. If I say Cindy Crawford is *a super model*, that means I think she's very good at what she does. If I call her *a supermodel*, that means she has transcended modeling and joined a special category. The distinction is more obvious with not-so-familiar *super*-terms: Call me *a super boss* and people who've worked for me would probably agree. Call me *a superboss* and you're saying a lot more. (This calculus need not apply to proper names such as *Super Bowl*.)

A SUPERB OWL? It's *Super Bowl*, OK? I don't know where *Superbowl* came from, but I guess it proves my theory that a complete lack of perspective on what should be one word and what should be two ranks right upthere—excuse me, *up there*—with the gratuitous use of double negatives and subject-verb disagreement as a telltale sign of illiteracy.

SUSPECT "SUSPECTS" Police like to throw the term *suspect* around when talking about killers, rapists, robbers, etc.—and so do reporters who either parrot police jargon or fear that the actual terms are libelous.

The word means, simply, "someone suspected of committing a crime." So if John Smith has been arrested in connection with a string of burglaries, it's entirely proper to call him a burglary suspect. The word is often misused, however, in crimes where there are no suspects.

If the only witness to a homicide saw the killer drive away in a blue sedan, the witness saw just that: the killer. Who, exactly, would the "suspect" be?

In fact, if someone has been arrested and you write about how "the suspect" shot the victims, you're libeling the person who has been arrested. The killer is the person who killed; the suspect may or may not be the killer.

In short, beware of the word. If substituting *the person suspected of committing the crime* makes sense, so does *suspect*. Otherwise, pick a different word (even the dreaded *perpetrator* would be better).

TACK, TACT The expression, derived from sailing, is *a new tack* or *a different tack*; it doesn't involve the word *tact*.

TEE BALL AND T-SHIRTS The little kids' version of baseball is *tee ball*, so named because the ball is hit off a tee. (What on earth would *T-ball* refer to?) The shirts that the players often wear are *T-shirts*, so named because they resemble the letter *T* when spread out. (What on earth would *tee-shirt* refer to?)

TELEPHONE NUMBERS The traditional use of parentheses for area codes is, as Martha Stewart would say, a Good Thing. Use (*202*) *555-1212* and not *202-555-1212* or *202/555-1212*. There's no need to make an exception for toll-free numbers to belabor the fact that *everybody*, and not just *most* people, has to add a *1* at the beginning. It's (*800*) *555-1212*. If you have to write *1-800-555-1212*, you darn well better write "*1-202-555-1212*, unless you're calling from the 202 area code, in which case it's just 555-1212, or from certain portions of the 703 and 301 area codes, where you could dial 703-555-1212 or 301-555-1212." See also 800 NUMBERS.

TENDINITIS A frequently misspelled word: It's not *tendonitis*.

THAT A misguided principle of the editing-by-rote school is to delete the word *that* whenever possible. It's often *possible*, but that doesn't mean it's *desirable*. Tin-eared editors chanting the mantra "Omit needless words" produce staccato ridiculousness that, in addition to sounding awful, can cause readers to stumble. Observe:

> *He declared his love for her had died.*

So you're reading along and you find that he declared his love for her. How sweet! Then you get to the end of the sentence and realize you've been misled. He declared *that* his love for her had died.

The kinds of sentences in which *that* must be preserved are too numerous to list, but a thoughtful editor will recognize when clarity is imperiled. Here's one common case: *President Clinton said Thursday he will sign the bill* is ambiguous—does *Thursday* refer to the statement or the bill-signing ceremony? He said Thursday *that* he will sign the bill.

Sometimes parallel construction dictates the use of *that*:

 WRONG: *The senator said his campaign will focus on the issues and that the campaign manager will not permit negative advertising.*

RIGHT: *The senator said that his campaign will focus on the issues and that the campaign manager will not permit negative advertising.*

THAT, WHICH *That* introduces essential clauses; *which* introduces nonessential (also known as nonrestrictive) clauses. If you have a hard time with that concept, here's a handy hint: *Which* clauses are always set off—usually by a comma, but sometimes by a dash or with parentheses. So your choice is between *that* and *comma-which*. If the comma seems out of place, *that* is your answer.

> *The City Council approved a program that will give Beanie Babies to disadvantaged children.* (*That*, with no comma, defines a newly introduced subject—in this case, the program.)

The program, which will cost $250 million, will start in May. (*Which*, with a comma, adds information about a subject that has already been introduced.)

Beanie Babies, which some people have dismissed as a silly fad, are simple plush toys but can sometimes command big prices. At the council hearing, one collector drew a distinction between Beanie Babies that continue to bear inflated price tags and Beanie Babies that anyone can buy at a toy store. (In general, proper nouns come with an established identity. A clause referring to them, as with the preceding "silly fad" clause, is by definition nonessential and gets the *comma-which* treatment, as in the first sentence in this paragraph. The second sentence illustrates an exception to that rule: A special distinction is being drawn within the established identity, and the introduction of new information that is *essential* to the meaning of the sentence requires the use of *that*.)

Some language commentators classify this distinction as a bugaboo, alongside the unsplitting of infinitives and the avoidance of sentence-ending prepositions. They're wrong.

"THE": SKIP ONE AT YOUR OWN PERIL Beware of sentences such as *Thousands are expected to visit the Gaza Strip and West Bank town of Jericho.* This implies that Jericho, as "the Gaza Strip and West Bank town," is somehow in both places. The sentence just needs another *the*, before *West Bank*.

TILL, 'TIL *Till* is a perfectly good word meaning "until." (In fact, *till* existed before *until*.)

'Til is a bastard child created through confusion—people heard *till* and assumed it was a contraction of *until*. Use *until*

in most cases and *till* when an informal touch is called for; never use *'til*.

TIME ELEMENT Mentioning when an event happened is vital, but reporters often get carried away. If a story for Wednesday morning's paper says something happened on Tuesday, there's no need to specify that the people commenting on the event are commenting on Tuesday.

TITLES AND COUNTRIES, ETC. Beware of constructions such as *Syria's Foreign Minister Farouk Sharaa*. Or *Foreign Minister Farouk Sharaa of Syria*. Those constructions attach the title to the name while divorcing it from the country—it reads as though the person's name is *Foreign Minister Farouk Sharaa* and he just happens to be from Syria.

The following alternatives all are acceptable:

> *Syrian Foreign Minister Farouk Sharaa.*
> *Syria's foreign minister, Farouk Sharaa.*
> *Farouk Sharaa, the Syrian foreign minister.*
> *Farouk Sharaa, Syria's foreign minister.*

As for U.S. elected offices, the same caution should be applied to *governor*, in which the state is vital to the meaning of the title. (Use *Virginia Gov. Jim Gilmore*, not *Gov. Jim Gilmore of Virginia*.) *Sen. John McCain of Arizona*, on the other hand, is fine, since he is not "the senator of Arizona," but a U.S. senator who happens to represent Arizona.

TITLES AND NAMES A basic tenet of journalistic style is that titles are capitalized only when they are used as a title directly before a name:

He had an audience with Pope John Paul II.
He had an audience with the pope.
U.S. Attorney Eric Holder denounced the verdict.
The U.S. attorney denounced the verdict.

In rare instances, a title can be both a person and an organization. For example, the head of the D.C. Corporation Counsel is the D.C. corporation counsel. The head of the U.N. High Commissioner for Refugees is the U.N. high commissioner for refugees.

TRADEMARKS How can anyone, let alone a professional writer, not know that facial tissues aren't *kleenex*, that soft drinks aren't *coke*, that photocopies aren't *xeroxes*? Part of being a writer or editor is having some awareness of the world around you, and such awareness should include the concept that, in most cases, generic objects in this world don't come with catchy names. I've seen a food writer refer to *ziplock baggies*, which not only desecrates two trademarks but also merges two competing big-name products into one generic whole, sort of like saying "Have a coke pepsi!"

As passionate as I feel about that point, however, I am far from being a trademark fetishist. Company lawyers will try to frighten you into believing that you can't use the names of their trademarked products without (a) capitalizing every letter, (b) following them with a ™ symbol, and (c) including the all-important generic identifier. In most cases, though, a single capital letter fulfills the journalist's obligation.

 IGNORANT: *They threw a frisbee around.*

RIDICULOUS: *They threw a FRISBEE™ brand plastic toy flying-disc product around.*

CORRECT (PROVIDED THE PRODUCT WAS OF THE
FRISBEE BRAND):   *They threw a Frisbee around.*

Companies with catchy names walk a fine line. The
Kleenex people *love* the fact that many people consider their
brand the "only" brand, but they live in fear because legal
precedent allows other companies to pilfer the word if it
becomes *too* accepted as a substitute term for the generic
product. I sympathize, and therefore I do what I can to honor
trademarks, but I refuse to allow my writing, or writing I've
edited, to look like a cheesy press release.

TRAGIC Don't participate in the dilution of the grand concept of tragedy. Yes, the dictionary will tell you that the third
or fourth definition of *tragic* is, basically, "bad." But do readers really need writers to tell them that a massacre at a high
school is bad? Leave the banal frowning, head-shaking misuse of *tragic* to the "Super-Duper Eyewitness Action News"
crowd.

TRANSPIRE The word is not synonymous with *happen* or
occur. An event transpires not when it takes place, but when it
becomes known. Even if you accept the contention that the
meaning has evolved, it's an awfully pretentious alternative to
happen.

TRASH, THRASH In a world where *dis* has become a household word, *trash* and *thrash* are often heard and often interchangeable. Both can mean "beat up," both can mean
"emphatically dismiss," and for that matter *beat up* can be used
to mean "emphatically dismiss." For what it's worth, though,
thrash is the better word for "beat up" (*McEnroe thrashed Con-*

nors in the 1984 Wimbledon final), and *trash* is the better word
for "emphatically dismiss" (*Siskel and Ebert trashed "I Spit on
Your Grave"*). It's a far better word for "destroy"—an extreme
version of "beat up"—which leads me to recommend: When
in doubt, use *trash*.

TRY AND Never, ever, use *try and* instead of *try to*, even if the
word *to* occurs 10 other times in the same sentence. I've seen
attempts by some language mavens to explain away this error
by saying *try and* implies a real hard try, and therefore success,
but they are wrong—if it's a successful try you're talking
about, why use *try* in the first place? *I'm going to try and build
a house* would mean the same thing as *I'm going to build a house.*

TYPE *Of* is often erroneously omitted.

 WRONG: *I wouldn't live in that type neighborhood.*

RIGHT: *I wouldn't live in that type of neighborhood.*

When a noun or an adjective is involved (rather than a
pronoun such as *this* or *that*) either the *of* construction or a
hyphenated substitute can work. Be aware, though, that the
noun or adjective often renders the *type* part redundant.

 RIGHT: *He lives in a ritzy type of neighborhood.*

ALSO RIGHT: *He lives in a ritzy-type neighborhood.*

BETTER: *He lives in a ritzy neighborhood.*

UNCLE, AUNT, COUSIN, ETC. Generally lowercase, but capitalize when used with names, as in *Uncle Mike and Aunt Ruth.*

UNITED KINGDOM It means Britain and Northern Ireland. *Britain* means England, Scotland and Wales. (*Great Britain* means the same thing as *Britain.*) So it's fine to refer to the United Kingdom in reference to a political issue that affects all of its parts or to say a company with locations in both Manchester and Belfast is a U.K. firm. But to refer to London or Liverpool or Brighton or Bognor Regis as being in the United Kingdom, while true, would be like saying *New York, North America.* Heck, even saying *Britain* is ridiculous if neither Scotland nor Wales is involved—what's wrong with saying *England?* Close your eyes and think of it!

UNIVERSITY NAMES Use *the,* but do not routinely capitalize it (regardless of what the letterhead says) when standard American English idiom calls for it in a university or college name:

> *He went to the University of Michigan, while she attended Michigan State University.*

If a university has multiple campuses, use *at,* and not a hyphen, comma or slash, to specify which one you're talking about:

> *She studied at the University of California at Los Angeles.*

UCLA might insist that it's *University of California, Los Angeles,* but that goes against the principle that writing ought to be readable—you wouldn't say "University of California [dramatic pause] Los Angeles." The comma works fine in lists or on letterheads, but in actual speech or writing, *at* is required.

If a university has just one campus, use *in*, not *at*:

> *The planetarium is at the University of Arizona in Tucson.*

Beware of misnaming an institution. Indiana University, the University of Notre Dame, the College of William and Mary, and the University of Kansas (with its dyslexic nickname, *KU*) are among those that often get turned around.

U.S. ATTORNEY'S OFFICE *U.S. Attorney's office* is a common capitalization error. Either you capitalize both *attorney's* and *office* or you lowercase both, depending on your publication's style on such entities. But, assuming you follow the Associated Press decree that titles are down unless they're used as genuine titles before names, *attorney* can't be capitalized all by itself.

I don't know whether this is a prime example of the widespread ignorance about that rule or whether it's a nod to the possible confusion that the naked *attorney* could cause— a U.S. attorney could mean simply a lawyer from the United States. I suspect it's a little of both, but I lean toward the ignorance theory, if only because *Attorney General's office*, a capitalization atrocity that cannot be attributed to a potential ambiguity, is almost as common. *Attorney*, of course, brings a long rap sheet to the court of usage (see ATTORNEY, LAWYER).

USED TO It's *I used to know how to spell*, not *I use to know how to spell*.

But don't point your automatic search-and-replace at *use to*: *Used to* is an idiom, but it still must obey the rules that govern auxiliary verbs. Just as *I had to do it* must become *I didn't have to do it* in the negative formation, *used to* must behave thusly:

 RIGHT: *He used to live in Phoenix.*

WRONG: *He didn't used to live in Dallas.*

RIGHT: *He didn't use to live in Dallas.*

VA There is no Veterans Administration anymore. It's the Department of Veterans Affairs. *VA* is still the abbreviation, however. So *VA hospital* is fine, but you should use *Department of Veterans Affairs hospital* in cases where you would have used *Veterans Administration hospital*. Capitalize *hospital* if you're referring to a specific hospital.

VIDEO GAME Two words.

VOICE MAIL It's not *voicemail*, no matter what the technologyhasnoroomforspaces crowd says. As a modifier, as with all two-word terms that many people consider one word, it must be hyphenated: *He changed his voice-mail greeting.*

VOILA A viola is a musical instrument. *Voila* is the French word that means something like "There it is!"

VOLLEY An exchange of shots in tennis or any other racket sport is a *rally*. A *volley* in tennis is a shot, other than an overhead or serve, hit before the ball bounces.

WHATEVER, WHAT EVER *Whatever* is correct when the meaning is "anything or everything that . . .":

Whatever happened is OK with me.

When *ever* acts independently from *what* as an intensifier of sorts, the expression should be rendered as two words:

What ever happened to Sargent Shriver?

Some dictionaries say the one-word form is correct in either sense, but the parallel example of *whoever* and *who ever* exposes the fallacy of that argument:

Whoever wants to do the job is welcome to it.
Who ever would do that job?

WHILE AWAY You *while* away the hours; you don't *wile* them away. (At least I don't.)

WIND CHILLS A subtle point, perhaps, but watch out for this local-TV-news affectation: "It's 40 below zero with the wind-chill factor." (AP, oddly, forbids the hyphen, but it's obviously needed here.) The wind-chill index (it's not properly called a *factor*) might be 40 below (and that's the way we should phrase it: *The wind-chill index is 40 below*), but "it" is still 21 or 72 or whatever the actual temperature is. The wind-chill number takes into account temperature and wind speed, but it doesn't *change* the actual temperature. The same rules apply to the "heat index," which takes into account temperature and humidity.

By the way, it's seldom, if ever, necessary to say *above zero*—if we say today's low is expected to be 2 degrees, that means above zero. If we meant below, we would have *said* below.

WITH AVAILABLE . . . This isn't something you're likely to encounter in a book or article, but please indulge my annoyance with this currently rampant quirk of ad-speak:

Instead of saying, quite correctly, that a car or truck or minivan is "available with anti-lock brakes" (or whatever), the announcer on a commercial will inevitably boast that it comes "with available anti-lock brakes." In other words, it *doesn't* come with anti-lock brakes, unless you pay extra. Heck, pay enough extra and you could get anti-lock brakes on your *dog*. They might as well advertise the Geo Metro as coming "with available Rolls-Royce."

(This is not to say the phrase is never appropriate. Add a relevant clause and it's fine: *With the available anti-lock brakes, the Geo Metro stops without skidding.*)

WORLD WIDE WEB, WEB, WEB SITE *The Web* (cap *W*) is acceptable on second reference and in informal references, but *World Wide Web* should usually be spelled out the first time. A site on the Web is a *Web site*. A web site is where flies go to die, and *website* is gibberish—it means the same thing as *zhoxtinj*. *Web page* is fine for describing a one-page site or a page within a site, but use *Web site* for multiple-page sites.

WORST—OR IS IT BEST? Call me sick, but I always chuckle when I hear about "the world's worst serial killer" or some such thing. The *worst* killer? I guess I'd be tied for that honor, since I've never killed anybody. Ted Bundy and Danny Rolling and John Wayne Gacy are among the *best* killers we know of, aren't they?

You wouldn't write *world's best serial killer*, of course, but *worst* just doesn't work. How about *most prolific serial killer*?

XMAS This is an abbreviation that, despite its legitimate history, should be avoided, because many Xians find it offensive.

YARD LINES The average football fan would call it the *50 yard line*, but those of us trained in matters of style tend to add a hyphen to the lineup: *50-yard line*. In this case, I think Joe Sixpack might have a point, or six or seven. In football's infancy, perhaps, those gradations were simply "lines" and there was a "10-yard" one, a "20-yard" one, etc. For as long as I can remember, though, those things have been *yard lines*, with 10, 20, etc. standing alone as their modifiers.

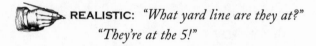 **REALISTIC:** *"What yard line are they at?"*
"They're at the 5!"

    UNREALISTIC: *"What line are they at?"*
"They're at the 5-yard line!"

An example of GRAFTING? Almost assuredly. But it's a clean break.

"YEAR 2000" PROBLEMS True or false: The year 2000 is the millennium. Most of my readers, I trust, know that the answer is "false." Now then . . . It's 2001, right?

Wrong. *No year* is "the millennium"! A millennium is a 1,000-year period. So 2001 is the start of a new millennium; it's the start of the third millennium A.D. in the Gregorian calendar; heck, it's even "A Space Odyssey"—but it's not "the millennium."

In case you're already lost, the reason the new millennium didn't begin in 2000 is simple. There was no year zero. So to count to the 1,000 years necessary to complete a millennium, you start at 1 and end at 1,000. The second millennium, therefore, began with 1,001, the same way the first one began with 1. For the same reason, the 21st century doesn't begin until 2001.

Now, I don't mean to pooh-pooh the significance of the year 2000. The psychological jolt of the end of the automatic *19-* was much more of a hurdle than the advent of the next millennium and the next century.

Speaking of which, there are two kinds of centuries. It isn't often that we split hairs so much when thinking about them, but there's century as in the 18th, the 19th and the 20th, and then there's century as in the 1700s, the 1800s and the 1900s. The year 1900 was part of the 1900s, but it wasn't part of the 20th century. So those seeking an "official" reason to hail 2000 could have called it simply the start of the 2000s!

Decades aren't typically given ordinal numbers, and so the *1900s* logic reigns. 1910 wasn't really part of the second decade of the 20th century, but anyone who was counting at that point no doubt stopped pretty quickly and succumbed to the simple fact that 1910 began *the 1910s*. By all means, 2000 is the start of the *decade* of the 2000s—I don't have an answer on how to distinguish that from the *century* of the 2000s; it's a slippery concept that was probably just as slippery in the *decades* of the 1700s and the 1800s.

Oh, and if you haven't already noticed, there are two *n*'s in *millennium* (and *millennia* and *millennial*).

And it's *the year* 2000, if for some reason 2000 alone would be confusing. It's not *the Year* 2000, even if you're referring to the computer glitch.

"YES, I HAVE" VS. "YES, I DO" I call this the Florence Henderson problem, because I first noticed it on "The Brady

Bunch." It's primarily a spoken error, but occasionally it might occur in print as well. Dialogue on the show would often go like this:

> *Greg: "Mom, do you have a minute?"*
> *Mrs. Brady: "Yes, I have."*

This usage, by the way, isn't confined to old situation comedies. I've never seen it discussed as a problem (please let me know if you have), but it drives me crazy. Mrs. Brady should have said, "Yes, I do." That's the way the "Yes, I [blank]" response works: [Blank] is the auxiliary ("helping") verb, not the verb it "helps." "Yes, I have" sounds OK to most ears because it's often used when "have" is the auxiliary verb. The following is a correct usage:

> *"Have you eaten the rest of the cake?"*
> *"Yes, I have."*

In the first example, however, *do* is the helping verb and *have* is the helped verb. Apply the same usage pattern to the second example and you get:

> *"Have you eaten the rest of the cake?"*
> *"Yes, I ate."*

The question, of course, wasn't whether person No. 2 had eaten; it was whether person No. 2 ate the rest of the cake. Imagine a "no" answer and the absurdity of *ate* becomes apparent: There's no getting around saying "No, I didn't."

Now for the subtle part. The following exchange may or may not violate my rule; you have to hear the way it's said to decide:

> *"Do you draw pictures?"*

"Yes, I draw."

Put the stress in the sentence on *draw* and the problem is apparent: *Yes, I do* would sound fine, but *Yes, I draw* doesn't. But in rare cases, as I said, the response in the example could work. If you put the accent on *yes* or *I*, then *draw* becomes a word that's repeated as a confirmation.

INDEX

ABOUT THE AUTHOR

Bill Walsh, copy desk chief of the Washington Post's business section, lives in the Capitol Hill neighborhood with his wife, Jacqueline Dupree. He was born in 1961 in Pottsville, Pa., and grew up in Madison Heights, Mich., and Mesa, Ariz. He received a bachelor's degree in journalism from the University of Arizona in 1984 and worked in a variety of reporting, editing and design positions at the Phoenix Gazette and the Washington Times before joining the Post in 1997. He has run The Slot: A Spot for Copy Editors (www.theslot.com) on the World Wide Web since 1995. This is his first book.